STILL TIME
for MIRACLES

STILL TIME for MIRACLES

Partnering with God to Perform Miracles

Yvette J. Smith

Xulon Press

Xulon Press
2301 Lucien Way #415
Maitland, FL 32751
407.339.4217
www.xulonpress.com

© 2022 by Yvette J. Smith

All rights reserved solely by the author. The author guarantees all contents are original and do not infringe upon the legal rights of any other person or work. No part of this book may be reproduced in any form without the permission of the author.

Due to the changing nature of the Internet, if there are any web addresses, links, or URLs included in this manuscript, these may have been altered and may no longer be accessible. The views and opinions shared in this book belong solely to the author and do not necessarily reflect those of the publisher. The publisher therefore disclaims responsibility for the views or opinions expressed within the work.

Unless otherwise indicated, Scripture quotations taken from the American King James Version (AKJV) – public domain.

Scripture quotations taken from the Holman Christian Standard Bible (HCSB). Copyright © 1999, 2000, 2002, 2003, 2009 by Holman Bible Publishers, Nashville Tennessee. All rights reserved.

Scripture quotations taken from the English Standard Version (ESV). Copyright © 2001 by Crossway, a publishing ministry of Good News Publishers. Used by permission. All rights reserved.

Scripture quotations taken from the Amplified Bible (AMP). Copyright © 1954, 1958, 1962, 1964, 1965, 1987 by The Lockman Foundation. Used by permission. All rights reserved.

Scripture quotations taken from the Complete Jewish Bible (CJB). Copyright © 1998 by David H. Stern. All rights reserved. No portion of this book may be reproduced, stored in a retrieval system, or transmitted in any form or by any means without prior written permission of the publisher.

Paperback ISBN-13: 978-1-66285-909-0
Ebook ISBN-13: 978-1-66285-910-6

Dedication

I dedicate this book to those who are in disbelief about miracles being performed today, those who haven't recognized various miracles that have taken place in their life, and those who will partner with the Holy Spirit as miracle workers to fulfill their destined purpose in the Kingdom of God. May God bless each of you on your journey with Jesus Christ and the Holy Spirit.

I bestow unspeakable praise and thanks to Yahweh and Yeshua for assigning me this work even before I knew it would be designated for me. I am deeply grateful that He continues to have need of me to fulfill His time-stamped purposed plan in my life and the life of others.

I also thank God for my mother who has always been an invaluable instrument of strength, stability, and solidarity for me. God has used her to impart wisdom and encouragement to help me navigate through the incredible ventures God assigns to me.

Table of Contents

Introduction ix
Chapter 1: Life Application—Personal Miracle No. 1 1
Chapter 2: What are Miracles and Why are They Relevant?........... 4
Chapter 3: Miracles as Visible Glory of God...................... 13
Chapter 4: Miracles as Signs and Wonders 20
Chapter 5: Miracles as Acts of Judgment from the Lord 31
Chapter 6: Miracles as Actions that Meet a Need or Complaint 36
Chapter 7: Miracles as Answered Prayer........................... 46
Chapter 8: Life Application—Personal Miracle No. 2 51
Chapter 9: Faith, Obedience, and Miracles are Interrelated 52
Chapter 10: Miracles Performed by Jesus.......................... 60
Chapter 11: Life Application—Personal Miracle No. 3 67
Chapter 12: Miracles Are Part of Your Purpose 69
Chapter 13: Life Application—Personal Miracles Performed 74
Chapter 14: Miracles are Kingdom Minded 77
Chapter 15: Timed Connection of Miracles......................... 83
Chapter 16: Partnering with God to Perform Miracles 88
Chapter 17: Your Miracle Journey................................. 93

Introduction

WHEN WAS THE last time you experienced a personal miracle that God specifically sent on your behalf to minister an answer or meet a need?

Do you remember the most recent occasion you witnessed someone receive a miracle that God delivered to them?

Miracles are very real and alive and are sent by God on a daily basis for all to acknowledge. My most recent occurrences of witnessing and experiencing miracles are from the daily events in my personal life and the life of others, and yours could be too. They aren't fairytales or folklore as many may presume, but a very natural part of our day to day life experiences.

Miracles are relevant today just as they were in biblical times. Signs, wonders, and miracles should never be contained to stories in the Bible, as they are part of our daily destiny. Unfortunately, many still don't realize that we, as believers in Jesus Christ, are all called to be miracle workers. This is a simple truth that Jesus mandated in how we were to carry on as His believers.

Miracles help to draw people to God—believers and unbelievers alike—so that He can be made known to all people in this world. They are necessary to bring about healing, deliverance, obedience, strength, endurance, and stability in everyday situations for a multitude of people. Miracles should be sought after and expected by everyone, especially in the times and seasons we live in.

As a believer, it's important to recognize that we have a responsibility to pursue God's miracles and work in collaboration with Him to perform miracles whenever and wherever He directs us. It's still time to embrace God's miracles, signs, and wonders.

Chapter 1
LIFE APPLICATION—PERSONAL MIRACLE NO. 1

Miracle at the Merry-Go-Round

IN THE MID-1970S, when I was about six years old, my mother took me and my older brother, John, with her to visit one of her friends who lived in an apartment complex. While we were there, my brother and I ventured out to the playground area, which had a vintage merry-go-round. At that age, I was in awe of everything my older brother did. If he did something, I wanted to be part of the action as well. During our time at the playground, my brother and I joined some other children by getting onto the merry-go-round. As the merry-go-round went around and around, I noticed that some of the older kids changed their seating positions. They were originally sitting properly and safely facing inward toward the center of the ride. Their legs were appropriately positioned inside of the ride while their hands were placed directly in front of their bodies allowing them to hold tightly to the bar in front of them. Then somehow the older kids changed from the correct seating position to then sitting in the opposite direction with their hands behind them holding onto the bar while their feet dangled on the outside of the ride. They did this position change while the merry-go-round spun around. After I saw that, I looked for my brother John and noticed that he too had changed his position. So, I thought it was okay for me to do the same, and I began my position change.

Something went terribly wrong when I attempted my position change. What appeared to be a cool transition for the other kids did not fare well for me. While the merry-go-round was still quickly spinning around, I remember turning my body around to position my legs on the outside of the ride and after that I blanked out and was unconscious. Minutes later, I awakened while lying on the ground in front of a huge steel streetlight pole, which had a very thick circumference. While I attempted to change my position on the ride, both of my hands released, and I flew into that thick pole. I looked up at my brother and was very confused as to what happened. I recall my brother, who is only eleven months older than me and was not that much bigger in size than me, pick me up and carry me to my mom's friend's apartment. My head was bleeding, and I was rushed to the nearest hospital.

Before I get into the other details about the accident, I want to point out a few things. Something supernatural occurred that day. Even though I did a very foolish thing, the Lord made sure to have His angels immediately show up on behalf of me, my brother, and my mother. The first thing is that having flown at unknown speeds through the air and hitting the thick steel streetlight pole head on, I was able to open my eyes and be fully alert after being unconscious for an undetermined amount of time. As you read this, you may not be able to capture the complete visual of the pole, but just know by all incidental rights, my six-year-old self should have died or been disabled. A miracle occurred in my life on that day for sure.

The second thing I want to point out is that my brother John, who will forever be my hero, was able to respond immediately to the incident by lifting me up and carrying me to safety. During his response, the Lord simultaneously provided him with supernatural assistance and strength to pick me up and run to the apartment. I will note that John lifted approximately his same body weight at that time, yet he didn't fail to get me safely to our mother. That was another miracle performed on behalf of me and our family that day. Without a doubt *Yahweh* (God) surely stepped in on time to ensure my life was spared and that I would be healed.

I went to the emergency room and had either a CT scan or an MRI of my head, and I recall the doctor telling my mother I was ready to be discharged home. The doctor said to my mother, in front of me, "Check on her often. When she gets up in the morning and you greet her, if she calls you 'Dad' bring her back to the hospital because it will mean she has brain damage." I don't recall what took place that evening when we got home, but I vividly remember the next morning. When my mother came in my room, I cheerfully and loudly said, "Good morning, Mom" with a big smile.

According to the National Institute of Health, children encountering traumatic brain injury is a leading cause of death and if the injury doesn't lead to death it can result in the child having cognitive, developmental, and intellectual delays or damage which can span across their lifetime.[1] I knew without a doubt when I woke up that next morning that I was healed, and brain damage had no room to exist in my life. This was yet another miracle God performed on my behalf. And I was, and continue to be, grateful to the Lord showing up on time for me.

Chapter 2
What are Miracles and Why are They Relevant?

What are Miracles?

IN TODAY'S TIME, many people are unsure of whether they have experienced a real miracle. Maybe it's the fast-paced nature of our lives that helps elude the fact that miracles happen on a daily basis in a person's life. It could also be that many people look for the grand display of a miracle, so they often miss the ones that appear to be normal or commonplace occurrences. Nevertheless, miracles are still present today just as in biblical times in which they are emphatically described and mentioned throughout both the Bible's Old and New Testaments. During biblical times, many people were aware that a miracle took place amongst them, while others may have missed them or chalked them up to nothing spectacular or extraordinary. Those who knew they bore witness to the miraculous events took it a step further and made sure to speak about the miracles in a reverent way to let others know that God was real and that He did perform signs and wonders on behalf of His people. If random people from biblical times were able to acknowledge miracles, then it could mean that they understood what miracles were and their significance.

It's my belief that there are various definitions or terms that illustrate the characterization of the word *miracle*. Miracles can be defined as an event or occurrence divinely orchestrated by God for you at a set time or moment in your life. Miracles can be described as the outward appearance of a

God-given answer or response that has been sought by a person. Describing and defining miracles can be very introspective and related to the words chosen by the person who has experienced or witnessed the miracle. This alone can lead to numerous definitions of miracles as each person who has witnessed or experienced a miraculous event may have varying ways of putting words to what they encountered. This is one reason why two people who witness a miraculous event can come away with a different take on the experience and whether a miracle actually happened or not.

Merriam-Webster's Dictionary defines miracles as "an extraordinary event manifesting divine intervention in human affairs."[2] In the *Strong's Concordance*, the Hebrew word *môphêth* (pronounced mo-faith) is used to signify the words *miracle, sign, wonder,* or *token* and is used multiple times in the Bible as a primary word of choice for miracles.[3] The Hebrew word *ôwth* (pronounced oth) also refers multiple times to being an appearance, miraculous signs, token, or miracle.

Below are just a few miracle descriptors that we will look at more closely in this book:

- Signs and wonders
- Visible glory of God
- An answered prayer
- Acts of judgment from the Lord
- Action that meets a need or complaint
- An event that aligns with God's purpose
- Actions taken by individuals to perform a sign and wonder

Creation is one of the first known miraculous events of all time. There's no question as to the majestic nature of God opening His mouth to speak words that then evocatively formed the entire world from nothing. Do you realize that every day you live and breathe, your existence is within the realms of a spoken creative and continuous miracle? Marvel at this, in Genesis 1, God produced an awesome phenomenon when He miraculously created the world and all of mankind. He didn't just haphazardly decide to perform that larger-than-life exhibition on a whim. He performed it with forethought, intentional purpose, and timing. When God spoke and performed miracles in the beginning of creation, He did so with wisdom and knowledge unknown to mankind. We must understand that

> **Miracles are always aligned with God's timing and His purpose.**

Genesis 1 is included here to help you visually appreciate that not only are you living within a perpetual miracle, but you yourself are a spoken miracle birthed out of God's words, wisdom, and time-generated purpose.

Genesis 1: 1-31
In the beginning, God created the heavens and the earth. The earth was without form and void, and darkness was over the face of the deep. And the Spirit of God was hovering over the face of the waters. And God said, "Let there be light," and there was light. And God saw that the light was good. And God separated the light from the darkness. God called the light Day, and the darkness he called Night. And there was evening and there was morning, the first day. And God said, "Let there be an expanse in the midst of the waters, and let it separate the waters from the waters." And God made the expanse and separated the waters that were under the expanse from the waters that were above the expanse. And it was so. And God called the expanse Heaven. And there was evening and there was morning, the second day. And God said, "Let the waters under the heavens be gathered together into one place, and let the dry land appear." And it was so. God called the dry land Earth, and the waters that were gathered together he called Seas. And God saw that it was good. And God said, "Let the earth sprout vegetation, plants yielding seed, and fruit trees bearing fruit in which is their seed, each according to

its kind, on the earth." And it was so. The earth brought forth vegetation, plants yielding seed according to their own kinds, and trees bearing fruit in which is their seed, each according to its kind. And God saw that it was good. And there was evening and there was morning, the third day. And God said, "Let there be lights in the expanse of the heavens to separate the day from the night. And let them be for signs and for seasons, and for days and years, and let them be lights in the expanse of the heavens to give light upon the earth." And it was so. And God made the two great lights—the greater light to rule the day and the lesser light to rule the night—and the stars. And God set them in the expanse of the heavens to give light on the earth, to rule over the day and over the night, and to separate the light from the darkness. And God saw that it was good. And there was evening and there was morning, the fourth day. And God said, "Let the waters swarm with swarms of living creatures, and let birds fly above the earth across the expanse of the heavens." So God created the great sea creatures and every living creature that moves, with which the waters swarm, according to their kinds, and every winged bird according to its kind. And God saw that it was good. And God blessed them, saying, "Be fruitful and multiply and fill the waters in the seas, and let birds multiply on the earth." And there was evening and there was morning, the fifth day. And God said, "Let the earth bring forth living creatures according to their kinds—livestock and creeping things and beasts of the earth according to their kinds." And it was so. And God made the beasts of the earth according to their kinds and the livestock according to their kinds, and everything that creeps on the ground according to its kind. And God saw that it was good. Then God said, "Let us make man in our image, after our likeness. And let them have dominion over the fish of the sea and over the birds of the heavens and over the livestock and over all the earth and over every creeping thing that creeps on the earth." So God created man in his own image, in the image of God he created him; male and female he created them. And God blessed them. And God said to them, "Be fruitful and multiply and fill the earth and subdue it and have dominion over the fish of the sea and over the birds of the heavens and over every living thing that moves on the earth." And God said, "Behold, I have given you every plant yielding seed that is on the face of all the earth, and every tree with seed in its fruit. You shall have them for food. And to every beast of the earth and to every bird of the heavens and to everything that creeps on the earth, everything that has the breath of life, I have given every green plant for food." And it was so. And God saw everything that he had made, and behold, it was very good. And there was evening and there was morning, the sixth day. (English Standard Version)

> **What is deemed a miracle to us is simply a divinely timed, purposeful event to God.**

You can see from the creation miracles that God performed many beneficial miracles, in fact some were even simultaneously completed. Those miracles can be expressed as marvelous signs and wonders, the visible glory of God, God exploits that met His and our needs, and an enormous event that truly aligned with His will and purpose. To God, these miracles weren't huge feats or miraculous events that were outside of His ability to perform but simply a result of His divine will and purpose being spoken out from the spiritual realm into the visible natural realm. On the contrary, to you and me, they are indeed a bounty of awe-inspiring wonders that we often marvel. God knew ahead of time that what He spoke and purposed to be would just be. He speaks it, and it appears and remains. That is an incredible lesson for us to implement as one of God's spiritual best practices when it comes to matters of miracles. We should exercise our God-given authority to speak and perform miracles in alignment with His will and His timing.

Relevance of Miracles

Given the times we live in, miracles are extremely relevant and discernibly needed by all. It has been mentioned numerous times over the years that we are living in the "last days." Each decade that goes by, people talk about the last days and what is yet to come as it is described in the Bible. The last days that were spoken about by the biblical prophets are indicative of the days and years that will end the time period that comes just before the beginning of the infamous last days. The last days relating to the last seven years that will occur just before the Great Millennium begins. The Bible warns us that during these last days, the times will be very troubling and we will witness and encounter people who reflect the following characteristics:

> 2 Timothy 3:1–5 (Complete Jewish Bible)
> People will be self-loving, money-loving, proud, arrogant, insulting, disobedient to parents, ungrateful, unholy, heartless, unappeasable, slanderous, uncontrolled, brutal, hateful of good, traitorous, headstrong, swollen with conceit, loving pleasure rather than God, as they retain the outer form of religion but deny its power.

This is a current snapshot of what we are now experiencing and living through, and the problem with this reality is that the times are promised to get intensely worse. Incredible amounts of evil will be present, like today, but even worse. In times like this we need the power of daily miracles. Only the power of the true living God can help us move through the daily challenges that lay ahead of us while unraveling the demonic intensities of evil that would attempt to overcome each of us.

Second Timothy 3 also informs us that even though we will endure persecutions God will fully equip us to be overcomers. God will also fully protect those who stay true to the teachings of the Lord Jesus Christ and who continue to practice what we learned from Him. Our faith and our steadfastness in Jesus Christ will equip us to maneuver through every test and trial. A portion of that maneuvering is the operation of miracles in which Jesus left us this promise in John 14:12–15 (Amplified Bible):

> I assure you *and* most solemnly say to you, anyone who believes in Me [as Savior] will also do the things that I do; and he will do even greater things than these [in extent and outreach], because I am going to the Father. And I will do whatever you ask in My name [as My representative], this I will do, so that the Father may be glorified *and* celebrated in the Son. If you ask Me anything in My name [as My representative], I will do it. If you [really] love Me, you will keep *and* obey My commandments.

> **You were born into this time, these last days, to pray for and encounter miracles.**

You are destined to speak miracles into existence because that is the greater work Jesus commissioned us into, along with the Holy Spirit, for us to take a hold of, embrace, and boldly walk out. Jesus healed people, delivered people from demons, and performed miracles like it was second nature to Him. We are made in His image and likeness, and because of that, He destined for each of us to operate in the different realms of the miraculous without giving it a second thought. Yes, you and me! That is part of our purpose and destiny.

We learned earlier that miracles are aligned with God's purpose and His timing. When God created each of us, and everything seen and unseen, He made provisions to include that His chosen people would walk around performing miracles that would benefit His people and the Kingdom of God. The miracles that were previously performed by God through ordinary people have impacted generations and many stories are shared and passed along about the power of the miraculous. We have so many examples of the miracles Moses performed, the ones God produced, the many that Jesus actualized, and countless other people that we may have never heard of as the centuries passed on. Each impactful story about the miracles experienced gets passed onto the next generation and helps increase spiritual faith in God's love for His people and should also encourage a more cherished relationship with Him. God left us a legacy of miracles that was never meant to lay lifeless or dormant but for us to be interactive with Him to activate miracles at every turn of our daily living.

Miracles produce strength, confidence, and obedience in both the worker of miracles and the one observing the miracle in action. In Exodus, when you read about how interactive Moses was with God in performing miracles, it's apparent that each miracle performed helped groom more confidence and strength in Moses. Confidence and strength are two attributes that caused Moses to develop a higher call of obedience to God and His commands. Examples are when God had Moses release the ten plagues against Pharoah. Those miraculous manifestations of plagues were a test of Moses' confidence in trusting God and relying on God's strength and ability and not his own. Those nine manifestations also required Moses to be timely, precise, and strictly adhere to God's plan. It's the same for you and me.

When operating as God's miracle worker, we must have an open ear to hear what God says and instructs while making the conscience choice to strictly adhere to what He said about how the miracle should be performed. When we closely align with the Lord, by following His instructions and commands, we see the miracles will effortlessly appear. God knows the timing that each situation and/or person needs a miracle, and He anticipates the obedient ones that will step up to the plate to be His ambassador to follow the prescriptive plan to release the miraculous. Our obedience can help bring about healing, supply, multiplication, and deliverance to many in need.

REFLECTIONS:
What are Miracles and Why are They Relevant?

Key Insights
1. Miracles are all around you every day. Look for them.
2. Miracles come in all sizes, shapes, and forms.
3. Miracles are answers to prayers and life changing events.
4. Miracles are always aligned with God's timing and His purpose.
5. The Lord intended us to operate in miracles, signs, and wonders as part of our destiny.
6. You were born to work miracles.
7. Be God's obedient partner to work as a miracle worker.

Chapter 3
Miracles as Visible Glory of God

Visible Glory of God

ONE NIGHT IN 2016 I woke in the middle of the night and saw a vision of a large burning flame that was suspended in the air. I laid in bed with my eyes open and saw the vision of the flame, which appeared to be at the level of a person's face if they were standing in my bedroom. The burning flame looked very large and real. I immediately knew it was either the presence of the Lord or an angel sent by God. The burning flame didn't scare me, but I was cognizant enough to be reverent of a Holy presence before me. Witnessing that vision, I realized something in my life was about to change even if I didn't know exactly what would change. Being able to see the presence of the Lord in that manner was another miraculous event in my life that I do not take lightly. It was a summoning for me into the next phase of my purpose and calling. When you are visited or encountered by a vision of fire, it is the Holy manifestation of God Himself divinely interrupting your normal way of life and existence to call you in deeper to His will, plans, and purposes.

> **Respect the flame and respond to it.**

Moses experienced a similar miracle when he was face to face with the burning bush in Exodus 3. The burning bush was the presence of God who spoke to Moses and ushered him into the next dimension of his life. Moses responded to the burning bush with a reverential fear and awareness that he was standing on Holy ground and was in the presence of *Yahweh* Himself. Moses responded to the message from the burning bush with agreement to the will of God for that new stage of his life. When we say yes to God, we all experience a commissioning and God may initiate that new place of duty by performing a miracle in front of your eyes, such as the burning flame in my vision or the burning bush that Moses experienced. None of us who yield to God in that level of reverence and agreement are exempt from experiencing Him in more intimate and intense ways.

In the burning bush commissioning, God called Moses out from the pattern of his day-to-day life into a much greater time-sensitive place that God preordained. Moses was designated to that burning bush experience since the day he was conceived and born for the intent to be used by God in saving a nation of people. That appointed commissioning was a spectacular, extraordinary, and powerful miraculous event of God showing up as a burning bush and was met with a stirring call and new assignment to send Moses out into a direction that would require him to further become one with God Himself.

> Exodus 3:1–12 (ESV) states:
> Now Moses was keeping the flock of his father-in-law, Jethro, the priest of Midian, and he led his flock to the west side of the wilderness and came to Horeb, the mountain of God. And the angel of the Lord appeared to him in a flame of fire out of the midst of a bush. He looked, and behold, the bush was burning, yet it was not consumed. And Moses said, "I will turn aside to see this great sight, why the bush is not burned." When the Lord saw that he turned aside to see, God called to him out of the bush, "Moses, Moses!" And he said, "Here I am." Then he said, "Do not come near; take your sandals off your feet, for the place on which you are standing is holy ground." And he said, "I am the God of your father, the God of Abraham, the God of Isaac, and

the God of Jacob." And Moses hid his face, for he was afraid to look at God.

Then the Lord said, "I have surely seen the affliction of my people who are in Egypt and have heard their cry because of their taskmasters. I know their sufferings, and I have come down to deliver them out of the hand of the Egyptians and to bring them up out of that land to a good and broad land, a land flowing with milk and honey, to the place of the Canaanites, the Hittites, the Amorites, the Perizzites, the Hivites, and the Jebusites. And now, behold, the cry of the people of Israel has come to me, and I have also seen the oppression with which the Egyptians oppress them. Come, I will send you to Pharaoh that you may bring my people, the children of Israel, out of Egypt." But Moses said to God, "Who am I that I should go to Pharaoh and bring the children of Israel out of Egypt?" He said, "But I will be with you, and this shall be the sign for you, that I have sent you: when you have brought the people out of Egypt, you shall serve God on this mountain."

When God comes to you in that manner, your natural inclination may be to become frightened and to second guess your abilities that God already has full confidence in. Many before you have felt that fear and inadequacy but that is more reason why oneness with God has to be worked on daily. Tasks, such as what Moses was enlisted for, can only be achieved by the intimate daily connective relationship with God, the empowerment of the Holy Spirit, and God's positioning of His assigned ministering angels. Moses learned to understand those concepts after he questioned God about his abilities and then listened to God's instructions and His assurances. God's responses to Moses were instructional about how Moses was to proceed in achieving oneness with Him. When we achieve oneness, we then capture the ability to render ourselves fully to the Lord's service because we embrace the reality that we are His true ambassadors in the earth and His image bearers. At that level, we understand that it is He, God, who operates through our earthly vessel at His will and pleasure. We give Him the rights to perform miracles, signs, and wonders through us whenever He wants to manifest them.

Other Visible Glory

Several times throughout the Bible, God showed up in a manifestation of visible glory. One of those instances was seeing a rainbow. How many times have you seen a rainbow in the sky? Some might say the rainbow is a response to weather or barometric pressure conditions. Others may stop and admire the beauty of how the rainbow forms a perfect arch with stunning colors. For me, I have had the pleasure to see rainbows at just the right moment when I needed God's reassurance of things that He promised me. At times I have seen double rainbows cast in the sky and again it was at the precise moment I needed a visible sign of God's glory to get me over some troubling obstacles in my life. Observing a rainbow in the sky is in fact a miracle manifestation of God's glory.

Genesis 9 details how God presented the rainbow as a sign of His covenant between the earth and himself. God spoke that covenant to Noah after the universal flood of the earth. It was God's promise to Noah, and those of us who would be born after Noah's time, that God would not destroy the people of the earth by universal flood again. The rainbow is an everlasting sign of God's everlasting promise and eternal covenant to His people that God promises never to forget Genesis 9:11–16 (The Complete Jewish Bible) states:

> I will establish my covenant with you that never again will all living beings be destroyed by the waters of a flood, and there will never again be a flood to destroy the earth." God added, "Here is the sign of the covenant I am making between myself and you and every living creature with you, for all generations to come: I am putting my rainbow in the cloud — it will be there as a sign of the covenant between myself and the earth. Whenever I bring clouds over the

earth, and the rainbow is seen in the cloud; I will remember my covenant which is between myself and you and every living creature of any kind; and the water will never again become a flood to destroy all living beings. The rainbow will be in the cloud; so that when I look at it, I will remember the everlasting covenant between God and every living creature of any kind on the earth."

This scripture is inspiring because not only can we look at the rainbow and remember God's covenant promise but also it tells us that God too can gaze upon the rainbow to call Him to remembrance of the covenant He made with mankind. That is spectacularly generous and loving of Him to do that for all of us. Just think, we may be gazing at the rainbow at the exact same time He does and be able to sense our connection and relationship we have with Him.

I often look into the sky at the clouds and the various formations clouds make. Sometimes I have seen faces of people, horses, dogs, hearts, an arm with muscles, a hand, and numerous other shapes and presentations. God uses the clouds to show us things He is saying or doing. Witnessing a pillar of a cloud is another instance of the visible glory of God. During the Israelites' exit from Egypt, God showed up in a pillar of a cloud that was a form of provision from the heat of the day for the Israelites. The pillar of a cloud also transformed to a pillar of fire at night to provide light to the Israelites and a sense of peace and comfort. In that miraculous manifestation, God traveled with the Israelites from Egypt through the wilderness and the Red Sea. In that miraculous form, God moved the cloud pillar from in front of the Israelites to behind them, so He could trouble and darken the path of the Egyptians who were in pursuit of the Israelites. God used those manifestations of miracles to show the Israelites that He would provide them with safety at every step of their journey. God does the same for us today.

In July 2003 I drove across the country from Delaware to live in California. When I drove through Oklahoma, the weather was sunny and clear but quickly became cloudy. Before I knew it I was under a gigantic cloud formation and had no idea what it was. The cloud spanned many feet wide and seemed to travel with me for many miles. I wasn't sure what it was, but I recall feeling curious but also safe under it. I don't believe I have ever experienced God's pillar of cloud, but that was the closest manifestation of it that my mind is able to comprehend. Years later, I came to understand that the gigantic cloud formation was in fact a thundercloud, a cumulonimbus, which can average to be fifteen miles wide and forty-thousand-feet tall, and sometimes can be indicative of an impending tornado or other weather condition. Just understanding those few facts alone, I recognize that God can do whatever He wants with His creation and become whatever He needs to be to get His message or destined plan accomplished. It is because of His ability that I can visually imagine that the pillar of cloud that led the six million Israelites could have looked like a cumulonimbus only much wider and larger. God manifested Himself in such a way that He placed a covering over His children every day without them being fearful or concerned about their escape route from Egypt into His place of safety.

Many of us have seen the visible glory of God, a miraculous observation, and may not have perceived it. Psalm 19:1-4 explains that all of us can see the glory of God on a daily basis if we can pause and recognize what is before our eyes.

> Psalm 19:1-4 (Holman Christian Standard Bible)
> The heavens declare the glory of God, and the sky proclaims the work of His hands. Day after day they pour out speech; night after night they communicate knowledge. There is no speech; there are no words; their voice is not heard. Their message has gone out to all the earth, and their words to the ends of the world.

Every time we look at the sky, we look at a portion of heaven and we get to witness miracles in the many forms and expressions of the visible glory of God.

REFLECTIONS:
Miracles as Visible Glory of God

Key Insights
1. Intimacy with God can usher in His glory.
2. The burning bush experience was a commissioning by God.
3. Respect the flame.
4. Take note of the visible manifestations of God all around you.
5. Be ready to witness miracles in your daily life.

Chapter 4
MIRACLES AS SIGNS AND WONDERS

Moses' Life Began with Signs and Wonders

GOD USED MOSES to perform an assortment of miracles to set the Israelites free from their bondage in Egypt. The miracles performed by Moses were considered signs and wonders, and acts of judgment. What was most significant about the miracles Moses performed was that they were released as part of God's divine timing to have the Israelites liberated from the Egyptian Pharoah so that God's will in their lives could prevail.

Let's take a closer look into Moses' life and how God pioneered him for the call as a worker of miracles, signs and wonders, and a deliverer of acts of judgment.

Moses' life began its earthly journey as a miracle as if it were foreshadowing his eventual call of performing miracles when the time came. Prior to the conception of Moses, a kingly edict went out to the Hebrew midwives with instructions to kill any newly born sons because the Egyptian king was fearful of being overpowered by the Israelites. At that time, the Israelites were rapidly conceiving and multiplying and the supervisor Hebrew midwives, Shiphrah and Puah, courageously refused to adhere to the mandate to kill any baby boys because they reverently feared God and not Pharoah. Pharoah, in his displeasure, released a decree to all his people that they should kill any Hebrew newborn sons by drowning them in the Nile River.

Moses' parents, Amram and Jochebed, were God-fearing people and they were very aware of the decree that was in place at the time Moses was born. Jochebed did what any mother would do to protect her child, she hid him for the first three months of his life. Jochebed, whose name means honor of God or God is glory, stayed true to the meaning of her name. She and her husband decided to put their full trust in God and had faith that God would protect Moses and direct their steps to secure his future. Hebrews 11:23 states that by faith Moses, when he was born, was hidden for three months by his parents, because they saw that the child was beautiful, and they were not afraid of the king's edict (English Standard Version). Moses' parents trusted that God would make provision to save their son and didn't allow fear to arise in them regarding what Pharoah wanted to do. Jochebed was able to conceal Moses' cries and sounds and likely hid him within her clothing and possibly amongst the household items when he wasn't nursing at her breasts. Essentially, Moses' birth and his first three months of life went undetected by any of Pharoah's men. God performed a timely and purposeful miracle because He had a plan for Moses's life.

Once Moses was three months old it became more challenging for Jochebed to continue hiding him under her clothing. He was growing, gaining weight, and becoming more active as is the growth pattern for any three-month old child. At that age, Moses could be seen moving his arms and legs around, attempting to grasp and hold objects, beginning to bear weight on his legs, turning his head to discover sounds, increased vision and eye focus, and many other milestones. It was at that point that Jochebed likely heard from God of what to do next in the efforts to save her son to ensure his destiny was secured. The Bible describes what Jochebed did in Exodus 2:3–10 (English Standard Version):

> When she could hide him no longer, she took for him a basket made of bulrushes and daubed it with bitumen and pitch. She put the child in it and placed it among the reeds by the riverbank. And his sister stood at a distance to know what would be done to him. Now the daughter of Pharaoh came down to bathe at the river, while her young women walked beside the river. She saw the basket among the reeds and sent her servant woman, and she took it. When she

opened it, she saw the child, and behold, the baby was crying. She took pity on him and said, "This is one of the Hebrews' children." Then his sister said to Pharaoh's daughter, "Shall I go and call you a nurse from the Hebrew women to nurse the child for you?" And Pharaoh's daughter said to her, "Go." So the girl went and called the child's mother. And Pharaoh's daughter said to her, "Take this child away and nurse him for me, and I will give you your wages." So the woman took the child and nursed him. When the child grew older, she brought him to Pharaoh's daughter, and he became her son. She named him Moses, "Because," she said, "I drew him out of the water."

God released another miracle at the very place where Pharoah condemned Moses and other newborn sons to die. God clearly gave Jochebed instructions on how to place Moses safely and securely in a basket and He caused that basket to flow down the river and be seen by the daughter of the woman He had predestined to raise Moses after he was weaned from his mother. God caused the heart of Pharoah's daughter to be impacted by pity and concern for Moses and in a miraculous turn of events had Moses returned to his mother so she could nurse him. But wait, Pharoah's daughter also paid Jochebed to nurse Moses, her very own son. Now that surely is a miracle! Jochebed didn't have to hide Moses any longer, she was able to bond with him and impart godly truth, wisdom, and teaching into him, and get paid for it. That means Jochebed likely had Moses for approximately three to five years based on Jewish and Egyptian customs before she had to give him over to Pharoah's daughter to allow the next phase of his life take place.

I have always believed God has a sense of humor as part of His personality and at times He expresses this humor to the point it often makes me say, "God sure has jokes." Look at this, Moses' life was sustained and prolonged on the very river that a death decree was set against him and other male infants. God performed a miracle on that same river, at the site of a death decree. Then God was so audacious to have it set up that Moses would be raised as a grandchild to the man that wanted Moses and other Hebrew sons killed. Later, Moses would perform a miracle at that same river. God certainly has humor, and He is too powerful to be messed with.

While Moses was raised as an Egyptian, he was fully aware that he was a Hebrew because he had been taught that by his parents before being turned over to live with Pharoah's daughter. He lived in Egyptian royalty and was trained to be an heir of an Egyptian kingdom, but God had other Kingdom-minded plans for Moses' life. When Moses became an adult, he was troubled by when he saw an Egyptian man kill one of his Hebrew citizens. This was so distressing to him that Moses acted in rage and killed the Egyptian. He immediately assumed his act of murder went unseen, but to his surprise he quickly found out from two Hebrew men that they saw him kill the Egyptian. When Moses realized the two men would undoubtedly report it back to the Pharoah, Moses took off running and fled Egypt. When he ran, he didn't have a second thought about the royalty and position he gave up because he knew he would have consequences to pay with Pharoah. Moses knew that Pharoah would either punish him or put him to death.

What about the consequences with God? Moses may have considered that he may have consequences to his sinful actions of murdering an Egyptian. At that point, Moses was likely aware that God called him to be a deliverer and he may have realized that his actions were very premature and ahead of God's time schedule of saving the Israelite nation. It surely crossed Moses' mind, especially since he was aware of his Hebrew heritage and the covenant he had with God. We will see later how God's redemptive plan for Moses played out.

When Moses ran from Egypt, he fled to a place called Midian which was miles outside of Egypt. Midian was a desert land without any designated boundaries, which offered Moses a place of solitude despite the Hebrew meaning for Midian being a place of strife or judgment. The word strife in the Hebrew meant to judge or govern, which is impactful because it is in the land of Midian where Moses learned that God appointed him to govern the future of the Israelites. Moses began a new journey and was able to openly embrace his Hebrew identity while living in Midian. For forty years he assumed a quiet and peaceful life there, where he married and had two children.

At the age of eighty, God knocked and divinely interrupted Moses' life and his daily routine because He had need of him. It was time for Moses to fulfill the call on his life. For countless years, the Israelites cried out to the Lord to be rescued from Egyptian slavery. Just like with you or me, there is an appointed time on God's calendar for us to be called into action for destiny. It was time for Moses' full purpose to be activated and what better way to get Moses' attention than to initiate him by way of a miracle? How many of you know that we all have a prescribed date to be called upon by the Lord to step into our divinely appointed time of action.

> **We are called ones with a responsibility to God's call to action.**

Signs and Wonders to Follow Believers

God bears witness to the salvation of people through a display of signs and wonders that are meant to confirm their salvation. Signs and wonders follow those who choose to believe through their faith that God can and will perform them. This is evident in Mark 16: 15–20 (Amplified Version), which states:

> Later, Jesus appeared to the eleven [disciples] themselves as they were reclining at the table; and He called them to account for their unbelief and hardness of heart, because they had not believed those who had seen Him after He had risen [from death]. And He said to them, "Go into all the world and preach the gospel to all creation. He who has believed [in Me] and has been baptized will be saved [from the penalty of God's wrath and judgment]; but he who has not believed will be condemned. These signs will

accompany those who have believed: in My name they will cast out demons, they will speak in new tongues; they will pick up serpents, and if they drink anything deadly, it will not hurt them; they will lay hands on the sick, and they will get well." So then, when the Lord Jesus had spoken to them, He was taken up into heaven and sat down at the right hand of God. And they went out and preached everywhere, while the Lord was working with them and confirming the word by the signs that followed.

As believers, we have specific mandates given to us by God the Father and Jesus Christ, to go forth announcing and proclaiming the gospel of Jesus Christ so that we may bring in the Kingdom's expected harvest of souls. When we allow God to use us as instruments of His glory to speak the Word of God and share our testimony, it will lead a portion of the unsaved to a new salvation experience. When someone who confesses their belief in Jesus becomes saved the Holy Spirit comes to live inside of the new believer after they repent of their sins. By faith, this then allows the door to open within the new believer for them to receive the baptism of water and the baptism of the Holy Spirit. Every believer needs those baptisms so they can be further empowered by the Holy Spirit so signs and wonders will follow them wherever they go.

The Apostles in the book of Acts were taught those concepts by Jesus and were instructed to go throughout the world teaching the same to everyone they encountered. Many of the true teachings are not taught today, which is why some may experience a new awakening by reading this book. Salvation through Jesus Christ is for all who choose to believe. Repentance is required by all who choose to believe in Jesus so God can blot out their sins and cause them to be made clean enough for His spirit to dwell and for His Kingdom's use in reaping in a harvest of souls. Repentance is necessary to be forgiven by God and to set proper alignment to work with Jesus and Holy Spirit on a daily basis. Once repentance has taken place, the baptism of the Holy Spirit can be imparted, and your fun and excitement can then begin. The

Lord can then assign you tasks for your involvement in spreading the gospel and having signs and wonders follow you everywhere you go. You may even witness seeing the people you evangelized about Jesus experience salvation, repentance, baptism, and the disbursement of signs and wonders of God's confirmation of their salvation.

> Acts 2:38–44 (English Standard Version) states:
> And Peter said to them, "Repent and be baptized every one of you in the name of Jesus Christ for the forgiveness of your sins, and you will receive the gift of the Holy Spirit. For the promise is for you and for your children and for all who are far off, everyone whom the Lord our God calls to himself." And with many other words he bore witness and continued to exhort them, saying, "Save yourselves from this crooked generation." So those who received his word were baptized, and there were added that day about three thousand souls. And they devoted themselves to the apostles' teaching and the fellowship, to the breaking of bread and the prayers. And awe came upon every soul, and many wonders and signs were being done through the apostles. And all who believed were together and had all things in common.

Jesus is very clear that the signs and wonders that follow us as believers are speaking in new tongues, casting out demons, picking up serpents and trampling them (Luke 10:19), recovery from drinking any poison, and laying hands on the sick so they may recover. We are also **warned not to neglect our salvation** (Hebrews 2:3–4) once we receive it as God Himself testified to our salvation and took steps to confirm our salvation through signs, wonders, miracles, and gifts given to us by the Holy Spirit. We should be people who are always sowing seeds in the harvest fields by determining to speak the truth of the gospel for others to hear and be in expectation that we will work miracles, signs, and wonders to those that choose to believe in Him. When we do this, Jesus, as our Great Intercessor, works with us to confirm the words we speak and makes sure to follow those words with signs and wonders.

Signs and wonders also are demonstrated so that someone will believe as described in John 4:46–54 (Holman Christian Standard Bible):

> Then He went again to Cana of Galilee, where He had turned the water into wine. There was a certain royal official whose son was ill at Capernaum. When this man heard that Jesus had come from Judea into Galilee, he went to Him and pleaded with Him to come down and heal his son, for he was about to die. Jesus told him, "Unless you people see signs and wonders, you will not believe." "Sir," the official said to Him, "come down before my boy dies!" "Go," Jesus told him, "Your son will live." The man believed what Jesus said to him and departed. While he was still going down, his slaves met him saying that his boy was alive. He asked them at what time he got better. "Yesterday at seven in the morning the fever left him," they answered. The father realized this was the very hour at which Jesus had told him, "Your son will live." Then he himself believed, along with his whole household. This, therefore, was the second sign Jesus performed after He came from Judea to Galilee.

As described in the scripture about the royal official and his sick son, Jesus released signs and wonders to not only trigger the royal official to believe, but also to make believers of those who were gathered in Cana of Galilee. Jesus had been in Cana previously for a wedding and, as you will read later in this book, the wedding party and the guests weren't aware of His first miracle. By the time of the scripture in John 4, news of Jesus had traveled about how He ministered to people and Jesus had come back to Galilee where He was incredibly welcomed. The people there were especially ripe for witnessing signs, wonders, and miracles.

The royal official heard Jesus would be in Galilee and he traveled there to see Him because he was desperate for his son to be healed. The royal official wasn't a believer when he met Jesus, but he petitioned Him for help because his son was nearing death. In John 4:48 (Amplified Version) Jesus replied to the royal official and the crowd of Galileans, "Unless you [people] see [miraculous] signs and wonders, you [simply] will not believe." The royal official seemed to brush off what Jesus said as if He was only speaking to the crowd and not him and pleaded with Jesus to come to his house right then or his son would die. When Jesus heard that, He told the royal official to go, and his son would live.

What would you have done if you were in that situation after hearing Jesus' response? Jesus' reply was very brief and simple, but many would have had an issue with hearing His response and think that He didn't address their concern the way they wanted it to be dealt with. Of note, the scripture states that the royal official believed. He heard the Word of the Lord and made a quick decision to believe what Jesus said and he traveled back about seventeen miles to his home in Capernaum. Many thoughts could have gone through the royal official's mind during that journey back home. Doubt could have come to snatch away the hope and promised fulfillment of his son's healing. How many times have you been given a promise of an expected miracle and you allowed your mind to flip flop around between belief and doubt?

The royal official had to make the decision to cast out any thoughts or imaginations that would let doubt and disbelief into his mind during that long seventeen mile walk home. Seventeen miles is just a little more than a half-marathon and if you have done a half or full marathon you understand that strength, stamina, and endurance are needed. You must be a focused fighter to complete the marathon and that is exactly what the royal official did on his journey home. He became a focused believer in an awaited miracle that he wasn't going to see manifest until he laid eyes on his son. He had to battle deceiving words or thoughts that were sent as an attack to get him to abort his belief in what Jesus proclaimed. The scripture lets us know that the royal official held tightly to belief in the word of Jesus and along his journey home some of his servants met up with him to let him know that his son was healed and very much alive. The servants let the royal official know that the precise time his son was healed, which corresponded to the time when the official heard Jesus tell him that his son would live. It was at that very moment that the royal official and his household became believers in Jesus Christ, the Son of God.

That example of encountering the Lord and holding onto His word with hope and belief is one we should embrace when we hear the Lord speak to us about matters concerning us. He will send signs to some of us and wonders to make us believe. Others may have to walk out a battle like the royal official to meet the signs and wonders. Some of us may have to press toward the miracle as if were a giant standing there blocking the entry, knowing that the only way to access the miracle was to slay the giant. We should aspire to never lose hope and belief in anything the Lord tells us. If He says that He is sending signs and wonders, then make a focused and targeted decision to believe Him no matter the cost. The cost could be steering clear of the naysayers in your family or your circle of friends. The cost could be ignoring your own mindset and way of perceiving your thoughts. The cost could be rebuking the voice of the enemy sowing weeds in your mind to cloud your ability to stay focused. Whatever the cost, trust that God won't let you down.

Reflections:
Miracles as Signs and Wonders

Key Insights
1. Your life is an expressed miracle.
2. God can use everyday occurrences to show you signs and wonders.
3. Don't neglect your salvation.
4. Signs and wonders help open the eyes of the unbelievers.
5. Miracles should lead people to God.
6. You may have to fight to meet up with the miracle.
7. Always trust God.

Chapter 5
MIRACLES AS ACTS OF JUDGMENT FROM THE LORD

Acts of Judgment from the Lord

GOD IS A very loving and patient God who is full of grace and mercy toward all people despite them doing good or bad deeds. Oftentimes, God will give us time extension after extension to help guide us back on track with our commitment to Him until He has had enough of the hardened hearts and blatant disregard for His holy authority. God's judgment can be seen through floods, storms, winds, earthquakes, plagues, and more. God, through Jesus, can release acts of judgment whenever He deems necessary. The Bible shares about many judgments that have occurred during biblical days and it also reveals about the future judgments that are yet to come. These judgments that are yet to come were prophesied long ago and will take place at a future date beyond the time of the writing of this book.

Many of us know the story about the Israelites' escape from Egypt by either reading it in the Bible or watching the movies that depict the great, spiritual, and historical event. As you read in the previous chapter, God chose Moses to work miracles of the plagues that were released against Egypt and their Pharoah so that His people, the Israelites, could be set free. In that case, time was up for the bondage and captivity the Israelites endured and God released judgment across the land. When Moses was enlisted for the mission to free the Israelites, the Lord told him right away that he would be sent to speak to Pharoah, but God was going to harden Pharoah's heart and make Pharoah cruel and irrational to deal with. Since God hardened Pharoah's heart, He promised that He would multiply His signs and wonders in Egypt.

Moses was God's representative who would solidify the manifestation of the ten plagues that God sent.

> Exodus 7:1–13 (English Standard Version) states:
> And the Lord said to Moses, "See, I have made you like God to Pharaoh, and your brother Aaron shall be your prophet. You shall speak all that I command you, and your brother Aaron shall tell Pharaoh to let the people of Israel go out of his land. But I will harden Pharaoh's heart, and though I multiply my signs and wonders in the land of Egypt, Pharaoh will not listen to you. Then I will lay my hand on Egypt and bring my hosts, my people the children of Israel, out of the land of Egypt by great acts of judgment. The Egyptians shall know that I am the Lord when I stretch out my hand against Egypt and bring out the people of Israel from among them." Moses and Aaron did so; they did just as the Lord commanded them. Now Moses was eighty years old, and Aaron eighty-three years old, when they spoke to Pharaoh. Then the Lord said to Moses and Aaron, "When Pharaoh says to you, 'Prove yourselves by working a miracle,' then you shall say to Aaron, 'Take your staff and cast it down before Pharaoh, that it may become a serpent.'" So Moses and Aaron went to Pharaoh and did just as the Lord commanded. Aaron cast down his staff before Pharaoh and his servants, and it became a serpent. Then Pharaoh summoned the wise men and the sorcerers, and they, the magicians of Egypt, also did the same by their secret arts. For each man cast down his staff, and they became serpents. But Aaron's staff swallowed up their staffs. Still Pharaoh's heart was hardened, and he would not listen to them, as the Lord had said.

Acts of judgment are designed to either harden a person's heart or bring them to a place of surrender to the Lord. God made seven demands of Pharoah through the words of Moses to let His people go. At each of those demands, Pharoah's heart grew harder. In fact, Pharoah's first paraphrased response to God's initial demand was "Who does the Lord think He is that I, Pharoah, should care to obey Him and let His people go." I don't know about you, but that level of disrespect is not something I want to ever verbalize to God. But God knew that was par for the course and what needed to be done to have the miracles in the form of plagues released, and what it took to free the people that He truly loved. Basically, Pharoah played right into God's hand, and he didn't even know it. It was like a chess match, and Pharoah was lured into God's plan without even realizing it. God had bigger intentions for the hardening of Pharoah's heart, which included demonstrating Moses' call as a miracle worker and ambassador of God, getting the Israelites to trust and believe God was real and always willing to fight for them, and bringing Pharoah and the Egyptians to their destruction.

God coached Moses along the way, but one thing He didn't tell Moses ahead of time was that Pharoah had magicians that were able to perform a few miracles. They weren't men of God. They were workers of Satan, as Satan does everything to mimic the power of the one and only true God. Those magicians, like Satan, had limited powers and were only able to change a rod to a serpent, turn water to blood, and make frogs appear. Interestingly, the magicians could not protect themselves from the plagues that God sent through Moses. That is a sure sign that it's always better to be on God's side where His divine protection and provision manifest because workers of iniquity will always meet their demise.

The ten plagues God unleashed on Pharoah and Egypt lasted for many weeks and Pharoah resisted the sovereignty of the Lord throughout all of them until the final plague's jolting blow. The final plague occurred during Passover when the Lord sent the death angel to kill all the firstborn Egyptians, which included Pharoah's son. The Passover is a holy time for the Lord and one of His best times to show someone who He is and what His people mean to Him. It was that final plague's act that broke Pharoah down, forcing him to yield to God's demands to let His people go. There's no safe place of refuge for you if you have hardened your heart against God or if God hardens it for you. Eventually, you will be brought to your knees before God takes you out. Pharoah had no choice but to concede to God. We can never expect to go up against God and win. It is best for everyone to repent and surrender themselves to the Lord Jesus Christ instead of contending with Him.

Reflections:

Miracles as Acts of Judgment from the Lord

Key Insights
1. Stay on the right side of God.
2. Acts of judgement are meant to soften or harden a person's heart.
3. Released plagues are miracles termed acts of judgement.
4. We can't expect to beat God.
5. Walk with God and receive His love.
6. God goes to war and fights for His people.

Chapter 6
Miracles as Actions that Meet a Need or Complaint

God Meets a Need or Complaint

IN EXODUS 16, Moses and Aaron journeyed from Egypt, through the Red Sea, and into the wilderness. While in their second month of the journey, the congregation of Israelites, millions of them, began murmuring and complaining that Moses had brought them into the wilderness to die. They complained that they were starving and didn't have any food or drink and they wished God would have killed them in Egypt. What kind of foolishness is that to say to the man of God who came to rescue you and to God after He just saved your lives?

The Israelites were a people known for constantly complaining the minute they had to engage in something that appeared to be deprivation or less than they intended or wanted for their lives. They were a people who cried out daily to God while they were enslaved and in Egyptian bondage, begging for Him to come save them despite them consistently disobeying His words and not living the way God intended. How many of us may behave like that on a regular basis?

Despite the Israelites ill babble toward God, He sent Moses to the rescue because He loved His people, like He does us, regardless of their shortcomings and He knew Moses was obedient and reliable. He led them on an overnight journey out of Egypt to the entrance of the Red Sea by providing them another manifestation of His glory, which was a pillar of a cloud that served as light for their path. The Bible states that the pillar of a cloud was positioned to cover the full company of Israelites and it appeared as darkness to them but it was brilliantly luminous enough to provide the entire Israelite camp with light so they could see where they were going.

I don't know about you, but I am awestruck. I know many of us have watched various movies showing the miracle at the Red Sea and the Israelites passing through it, but maybe we can't fully appreciate what took place because the depictions don't reveal how long the escape took. Once Moses and the Israelite camp arrived at the Red Sea, Exodus 14:21 (Authorized King James Version) states, "Moses stretched out his hand over the sea; and the LORD caused the sea to go back by a strong east wind all that night, and made the sea dry land, and the waters were divided. And the children of Israel went into the midst of the sea upon the dry ground: and the waters were a wall unto them on their right hand, and on their left."

At that point in time, it is my estimation that Moses and the Israelites may have been traveling since 6 p.m. the night before getting to the Red Sea and once there the east wind blew all night long, keeping the sea parted. As they were passed through the parted sea, the Egyptians pursued them but had not quite caught up to them and then God stepped in again on behalf of His chosen in Exodus 14:23–25 (Authorized King James Version) which states:

> And the Egyptians pursued and went in after them to the midst of the sea, even all Pharaoh's horses, his chariots, and his horsemen. And it came to pass, that in the morning watch the LORD looked unto the host of the Egyptians through the pillar of fire and of the cloud and troubled the host of the Egyptians, and took off their chariot wheels, that they drave them heavily: so that the Egyptians said, Let us flee from the face of Israel, for the LORD fighteth for them against the Egyptians .

According to Dake's Annotated Reference Bible, the morning watch relates to the hours between 3am to 6pm and is known as the fourth watch of the night.[4] This time of the night is known as the last watch of the night where you pray and intercede to establish your day and listen to the Lord for instructions on what is to happen in your day. This time period is when prayer stops the planned activity of the enemy.

God directed Moses in one of the most grandiose miracles known today by instructing him to stretch out his hand over the Red Sea to supernaturally cause it to split. During this act of splitting the sea the Lord, through Moses, created a one-hundred-foot tall frozen sea wall that kept the waters from drowning the Israelites and the multitude of mixed people. The people, according to Dake's Annotated Reference Bible, totaled approximately six million and the Lord caused them to divinely walk on a well-defined twelve mile path of dry sea bed to safety, all while being ferociously pursued by an army of Egyptians and their horses and chariots.

The entire detail of that miraculous event speaks volumes about the unrelenting compassion God had for the Israelites. How remarkable it must have been to have encountered the events leading to this miracle while also being an active viewer of the miracle. It's simply mind-blowing. Then to complement the magnificence of the Red Sea escape, God made the sea floor become dry and held back the water so the Israelites could walk through. Once they were at a safe distance and He saw the Egyptians encroaching, God instructed Moses on stretching his hand over the sea again so that by the time morning appeared, the 100 foot high wall of water instantly melted. The instantaneous melting of the frozen sea wall triggered the waters to swallow up all the Egyptians that were running through the sea to kill the Israelites.

It can be said that during that specific moment of the Exodus passage, Moses worked very closely with God for approximately eighteen hours or more.[5] Moses was responsible for spearheading a warring escape from Egyptian bondage by leading the company of six million Israelites and mixed people, along with their livestock and treasures, to a safe land. God never once left their sides because their salvation was at stake and was very essential to Him.

I have always been curious how the Israelites could go through such a mind blowing and life changing experience. An experience that was most likely very frightening yet they were able to endure it and acknowledge the miracle by going into song, dance, and beautiful praise to the Lord God Almighty immediately after they crossed through the Red Sea. However, within two months post-miracle, they became stalemated enough in their thinking to perceive they were starving and forget that God is Jehovah Jireh and would take care of them. I've been curious how they could forget what God did for them two months prior. Sixty whole days is all it took for six million people who witnessed the most miraculous event in history at that time to lose sight and forget what God had just wondrously performed on their behalf. All of a sudden, they didn't think that God would bless them with food to eat and water to drink. Those six million people didn't have trust or belief that God would not allow them to starve or die of hunger in the wilderness.

That is also many of us today. We can easily lose sight of the valuable experience and miracle we encountered with God if we focus on the lack of fulfillment for our immediate desires. While the Israelites were enslaved in Egypt, although they complained to God, they didn't seem to lose focus that God would rescue them because they were able to enjoy food and the pleasures of their day after working hard every day. They weren't aware that in order to be saved they would have to give up their routines to follow God. They weren't aware that He would still take care of them with what He knew was good for them and that they would enjoy what He supplied. What happened two months after passing through the Red Sea was that approximately six million people wanted to have comfortable pain which they equated to pleasure, instead of an unpredictable new pain and temporary suffering. In essence, those six million people, just like many of us today, didn't want to give up their old ways, mindsets, traditions, pleasures, and routines to trust God for everything that came in their present and future.

The Israelites were only meant to pass through the wilderness to get to the Promised Land that God told them about, but they didn't have enough faith or trust in the Lord's guidance. They also didn't have the vision to see or believe in the future the Lord was bringing them into so they began their toddler behavior of temper tantrums and complaining to attempt to sway God's plan for them. Here is a lesson learned from the Israelites: Sometimes our complaining and toddler-like behavior forces God to plant us where He never wanted us to be planted because our actions and behavior prevent Him from moving us into our promise.

In response to the constant grumbling, the Lord appeared before them in a cloud that revealed His glory, and He delivered a word through Moses and let those six million men, women, and children know that God heard their complaints and would provide daily miracles of food to eat. God told them He would meet their daily needs for food by sending quail in the evening and He would rain down manna from heaven every morning. I want you to appreciate this miracle God performed by sending enough quail that appeared out of nowhere to feed six million people every single evening while they were in the wilderness for forty years. Quail is a delicacy that tastes better than chicken and it has nutritionally healthy benefits from vitamins, minerals, and macronutrients to supply the body with what it needs while also helping keep a body's bones strong. God knew exactly what He was doing by sending the Israelites that delicacy. He knew the human body needed strength and nutrients, especially when engaged in a wilderness experience.

Manna was a new phenomenon and food provision that the Israelites had never known until they arrived in the wilderness. It was angel's food from heaven as noted in Psalm 78:25 and it had a rich creamy taste. When God rained down the manna, He did so in a fashion that He sent the morning dew first so it would cool down the ground because He didn't want any of the manna to dissolve before the six million people could gather it for their morning bread. That means there was a protocol to the provision and release of the double miracle. Manna, by design, couldn't supernaturally appear until the supernatural dew had completed its job because God didn't want any of the manna, the daily bread, to go to waste. God took care of every detail while simultaneously taking care of the daily needs of His grumbling people. God sent the manna daily to help the six million members of the Israelite camp understand that they were to spend time with Him daily, be grateful in worship, and recognize that He was a God who would fulfill their needs. He wanted them to understand there was no need to doubt Him or complain about what they felt they were lacking. God wanted them to know that they could develop a trusting relationship with Him while also following His instructions and He would continue to provide surety for their present and their future for generations to come.

> **Many don't see miracles as blessings because they are so focused on how those miracles interrupt their ways of doing things.**

Like the Israelites, we too have to be shown miracles on a daily basis, but it is up to us to be aware and recognize that God produces and sends us miracles every day. God made it very easy and convenient for six million people, to the point they didn't have to toil with the ground to get their food or worry about what food they would eat tomorrow. God provided everything they needed and all they had to do was be reverent of Him and recognize the spiritual lessons He taught. Somehow, they missed the boat in learning and obeying His ways, and I believe it was because they wanted to control their own storyline just like many of us do today. Many attempt to control and manipulate God and that's exactly what happened in the Israelites' forty-year wilderness experience.

We must be careful with our response to miracles, accept the timing and purpose of each miracle, and process what God wants us to glean from miracles. I think it is critical to highlight Numbers 11, which shows how the Israelites failed to give the right response and had the wrong perspective of the miracles that God wanted them to have.

Numbers 11: 1-15 (English Standard Version) states:
And the people complained in the hearing of the Lord about their misfortunes, and when the Lord heard it, his anger was kindled, and the fire of the Lord burned among them and consumed some outlying parts of the camp. Then the people cried out to Moses, and Moses prayed to the Lord, and the fire died down. So the name of that place was called Taberah, because the fire of the Lord burned among them. Now the rabble that was among them had a strong craving. And the people of Israel also wept again and said, "Oh that we had meat to eat! We remember the fish we ate in Egypt that cost nothing, the cucumbers, the melons, the leeks, the onions, and the garlic. But now our strength is dried up, and there is nothing at all but this manna to look at." Now the manna was like coriander seed, and its appearance like that of bdellium. The people went about and gathered it and ground it in handmills or beat it in mortars and boiled it in pots and made cakes of it. And the taste of it was like the taste of cakes baked with oil. When the dew fell upon the camp in the night, the manna fell with it. Moses heard the people weeping throughout their clans, everyone at the door of his tent. And the anger of the Lord blazed hotly, and Moses was displeased. Moses said to the Lord, "Why have you dealt ill with your servant? And why have I not found favor in your sight, that you lay the burden of all this people on me? Did I conceive all this people? Did I give them birth, that you should say to me, 'Carry them in your bosom, as a nurse carries a nursing child,' to the land that you swore to give their fathers? Where am I to get meat to give to all this people? For they weep before me and say, 'Give us meat, that we may eat.' I am not able to carry all this people alone; the burden is too heavy for me. If you

will treat me like this, kill me at once, if I find favor in your sight, that I may not see my wretchedness."

God then sent Moses' help in the form of strong men who God placed His Spirit in and then in Numbers 11 verses 31-35, He sent another miraculous response to the consistent murmuring. That was not a response from God any of us should aspire to receive. Be careful of what you say in the Lord's hearing so that you don't kindle His anger against you resulting in a plague.

> Numbers 11:31-35 (English Standard Version) states:
> Then a wind from the Lord sprang up, and it brought quail from the sea and let them fall beside the camp, about a day's journey on this side and a day's journey on the other side, around the camp, and about two cubits above the ground. And the people rose all that day and all night and all the next day and gathered the quail. Those who gathered least gathered ten homers. And they spread them out for themselves all around the camp. While the meat was yet between their teeth, before it was consumed, the anger of the Lord was kindled against the people, and the Lord struck down the people with a very great plague. Therefore the name of that place was called Kibroth-hattaavah, because there they buried the people who had the craving. From Kibroth-hattaavah the people journeyed to Hazeroth, and they remained at Hazeroth.

We should all be cautioned about murmuring, complaining, and grumbling about the situations we encounter, especially when we feel like we don't have enough of God's goodness in our life. Or thinking or believing God should be doing more for us than He planned because God hears everything that is thought or spoken. You must be mindful and consider what you have moaned and groaned about in the Lord's presence. What do you accuse Him of that is not His fault? What miracles has He sent to you that you said didn't meet your need? What blessings has He given that you have rejected or discarded and not acknowledged?

As you have read, God tolerates the mumbling and complaining for a bit, but after a while it became a filthy irritant to Him and made Him angry. Surely, we should not desire to cause Him to strike out against us just to have our bellies full or every whimsical fleshly desire satisfied. We also should not aspire to have our movement forward stalled because we don't understand where He is moving us. Don't have God send a manna miracle when He intended to give you a milk and honey miracle. Don't stop your growth and box in His level of miraculous provision He wants to pour out.

Reflections:
Miracles as Actions that Meets a Need or Complaint

Key Insights
1. God can send miracles to meet your needs.
2. Complaining and murmuring can spark the anger of the Lord.
3. Don't reject the miracles God sends.
4. Respond to God with gratitude for the timing and purpose of His miracles.
5. Expect God's original miracle.
6. Don't stall God's plans for your life by grumbling and complaining.
7. Desire the milk and honey miracle.

Chapter 7
MIRACLES AS ANSWERED PRAYERS

Answered Prayers are Synonymous with Miracles

GOD TAKES PLEASURE in hearing from us and answering our prayers. Additionally, Jesus is our intercessor, and He often goes to God the Father on our behalf so that we may be helped and blessed. Miracles can be a form of God's response to our prayers.

God gives us multiple promises in the Bible about Him answering our prayers. These promises are endearing, true, and everlasting.

> 1 John 5:14–15 (English Standard Version) states:
> And this is the confidence that we have toward him, that if we ask anything according to his will he hears us. And if we know that he hears us in whatever we ask, we know that we have the requests that we have asked of him.
> John 15:7 (English Standard Version) states:
> If you abide in me, and my words abide in you, ask whatever you wish, and it will be done for you.
> Matthew 21:22 (English Standard Version) states:
> And whatever you ask in prayer, you will receive, if you have faith.
> John 15:16 (English Standard Version) states:
> You did not choose me, but I chose you and appointed you that you should go and bear fruit and that your fruit should

abide, so that whatever you ask the Father in my name, he may give it to you.
Isaiah 65:24 (English Standard Version) states:
Before they call I will answer; while they are yet speaking I will hear.

God chose us to enter viable relationships with Him. He welcomes the time we spend with Him and encourages us to trust Him and regularly talk to Him. He hears us when we speak and already has an answer waiting for us before we finish our prayer, intercession, or conversation. One major takeaway from His promises is that we should walk in assured confidence in Him and His ability to answer our questions and supplications.

Throughout your life you may remember times you or others submitted prayer requests to the Lord on your behalf to change a situation and receive what you now know is a miracle. We may take those times for granted and assume that God never replied. We may think nothing was done about our requests. That perception could be based on numerous factors. One primary reason is chalking up the occasion to you not receiving an immediate answer or believing when the answer arrived, the actual miracle, it wasn't noteworthy enough to you at the time it came. Sometimes, in the busyness of our days, we can forget the requests we pled to the Lord. Sometimes we can become angry at God and think He forgot us and didn't respond when we felt we needed Him the most. The scriptures you just read show that He will always answer us. The key is that we must know what to look for in God's answer.

Too often we want a miracle based on what our carnal-minded standards can distinguish. We expect the miraculous answer to our prayer to check off the boxes of our internally constructed and defined thoughts, which leaves no room for God to be God and send the miracle He knows is fitting for our situation. There are times that we can't get our mind to stretch outside of our worldly conceived framework, which limits our spiritual view of what God can supernaturally do for us. We must be incredibly careful not to control God's miracles with our own thoughts and perceptions of what God wants to do for us when we make our requests known to Him. We should adopt the attitude of Daniel 3:17–18 (Authorized King James Version), which states:

> If it be so, our God whom we serve is able to deliver us from the burning fiery furnace, and he will deliver us out of thine hand, O king. But if not, be it known unto thee, O king, that we will not serve thy gods, nor worship the golden image which thou hast set up.

Becoming fully aware that a miracle was sent as an answer to our prayers and intercessions requires us to have transformed and renewed minds. It mandates that we have our vision and hearing enlightened by the Holy Spirit so we can connect with God in a more heavenly way, and so we don't miss what He does on our behalf.

Recognizing a miracle as an answer to prayers also demands that we exercise faith. Faith without works is dead and if we have no faith for what we ask God for, then it becomes impossible to please God, let alone receive from Him. The Bible tells us that we are to pray without ceasing, so while we wait for miraculous answers, we must continue to pray and walk in faith that we will receive what we asked from God. We must envision our requests as answered, and it will soon come. Remember that God takes pleasure in answering His people.

> **Sending miracles, signs, and wonders is His specialty.**

We have to be cognizant of the arrival of the signs.

If you keep a journal of your prayer requests that illustrates when your prayers were answered, those requests could possibly get lost in multiple journal books or forgotten about over time. It is a beneficial practice to regularly review your prayer requests and conversations you have with God and then document the associated answer or miracle He sent, along with the form the miracle came in. This can help be a visualized path forward in knowing the ways of the Lord. Performing this practice will also help you recognize His miracles on your behalf and can help activate your faith and trust in Him while encouraging a deeper walk and testimony that can be shared with others. Every miracle you experience because of God answering your prayers is a point of reference to share with others to bring them hope and evidence that God is very much real. What He does for you He can do others. That is how He rolls.

Reflections:
Miracles as Answered Prayers

Key Insights
1. Answered prayers are miracles.
2. Faith is required for you to recognize answered prayers as miracles.
3. Miracles as answered prayers may not come the way we think they should.
4. Transform and renew your mind to make room for the miracles God sends.
5. God hears your prayers as soon as you speak them.
6. God will always answer your prayers if you believe.
7. Record your prayers and the miracles God sends.

Chapter 8
Life Application: Personal Miracle No. 2

I'VE KEPT A journal for many years to record words and dreams the Lord has given me, as well as some of my prayer requests. Throughout the hundreds of pages of journal notes I have recorded, and from things I can personally recall, God has shown Himself as a miracle worker in my life.

The Lord has answered many prayers of provision for me, countless times, through manifestations of sending financial resources, opening doors for jobs, authorizing bonuses or increased income that were outside of my standard bracket. He removed roadblocks and obstacles that attempted to prevent me from purchasing several homes. He answered my prayers for healing either by divinely healing me or causing another to lay hands on me to receive healing. God allowed me to see in the heavenlies and see His majestic signs in the skies. There's so much that God has done for me in the form of miracles, signs, and wonders as answers to my prayers for myself and others.

I have learned over the years to trust God and His ways. Whether I am praying for myself, others, or even you, I have enough faith to know that He will perform miracles on behalf of the intercession. He will send His signs and wonders as answers to give hope, reassurance, provision, and salvation. He's done it time and time again and I will continue to look for and accept the miracles He sends.

What answers to prayers have you received that you can now say were miracles sent by God?

Chapter 9
Faith, Obedience, and Miracles are Related

More Faith and Obedience

It's interesting to see in the *Strong's Concordance*[3] that the Hebrew word *môphêth*, which translates to miracle, uses the word faith and can even be stated as "more faith" since faith is an integral component of performing miracles. It's already known from scripture that God gives everyone a measure of faith and that without faith it is impossible to please God. If we don't have enough faith, we can ask the Holy Spirit for the gift of faith, which is one of His powers that He bestows at will or when we ask for the gift. Having faith is key to operating in miracles. Faith must simultaneously operate with God's timing and purpose for the intended miracle.

The Israelites who were saved by God's miracles didn't have the faith to see how He operated and it forced them to walk in doubt and disbelief for forty years. Once they went through the Red Sea experience into the wilderness in Sinai, they made a conscious choice to settle into distrust and skepticism about God and that cost them forty years of redundancy instead of receipt of God's intended plan and promise for their lives. Doubt and disbelief blurs faith and washes away trust while breeding the presence of doublemindedness, hopelessness, and fear. Those were the conditions the Israelites were affected by during their stay in the wilderness.

At the first month of the fortieth year after God rescued the Israelites from Egypt, they still had no faith to move past the wilderness into the promised placed God told them about. They spent forty years in a wilderness that they were only meant to stay a few days in. They were stuck. As a result, many of the older generations died, so they never entered the fulfillment of God's promise. Coincidentally, the newer generation learned the unpleasant habits of disbelief and fear from their predecessors. In Numbers 20:1–5 (Holman Christian Standard Bible) they continued murmuring and complaining based on the conditions of their corruptible mindsets:

> The entire Israelite community entered the Wilderness of Zin in the first month, and they settled in Kadesh. Miriam died and was buried there. There was no water for the community, so they assembled against Moses and Aaron. The people quarreled with Moses and said, "If only we had perished when our brothers perished before the Lord. Why have you brought the Lord's assembly into this wilderness for us and our livestock to die here? Why have you led us up from Egypt to bring us to this evil place? It's not a place of grain, figs, vines, and pomegranates, and there is no water to drink!"

The new generation used the same complaining and murmuring that God despised in the former generation. Complaining and murmuring emits a foul odor to God's nostrils and He considered this new generation to be of little faith and unable to please Him because of their mindset. They were a malodorous generation of unbelievers who emanated a funky stench in the Lord's presence because they refused to trust and believe in Him and depend on His protection despite every miracle He performed. How many people do you know who operate that way? Do you have little to no faith or belief in doing what God wants to do through you? Lack of faith and no belief is a disastrous combination for trusting in anything that God has for you. That combination will paralyze you, as if your arms and feet are sealed in cement. It forces your mind to be stagnant and you'll always live in the past of when you thought your life was better than where God wants you to go. Zero faith and no belief won't allow you to move forward, and that is really what God wants all of us to do…MOVE forward with Him.

Letting the stinking thinking of the past occupy your mind is a perilous place to reside and even more dangerous for it to be taught to the next generation. Nothing good can come of stinking thinking unless you repent and let God transform your mindset and lead you daily. The Israelites wanted their own way and when they didn't get it, they moaned with a spirit of manipulation and rebellion reasoning that their actions would move the Lord in their direction. We can't treat the Lord like a genie in a bottle. We can't serve Him fully and continue in our own ways, despite what many may think or feel. Serving the Lord fully and continuing in your own way is like oil and water and they don't mix with His intended plans for us. God continues to look for obedient and faithful people who will go the distance to complete their heavenly assignments. We need faith and obedience to do so.

Throughout the Bible, we are warned to get rid of disbelief and to have faith. God can't do much with us as Kingdom people if we hold onto disbelief. When a person's heart is hardened by disbelief, it prevents the movement of miracles and healings because the disbelief, in essence, rejects the Holy Spirit's liberty to move on behalf of people. God is very generous and kind to us by orchestrating that if we know we are rooted in unbelief, we can REPENT and cast it out of us by adopting the spirit of belief. As you read God gave each of us a measure of faith. Some of us have more than others. If you are lacking faith, you can ask God to change your perspective about faith and He will do that. The goal is to utilize the faith that God embedded in you, and that comes from acknowledging Him and His truths and partnering with Him through your obedience.

> Matthew 17:20 (Authorized King James Version) states:
> Then came the disciples to Jesus apart, and said, Why could not we cast him out? And Jesus said unto them, Because of your unbelief: for verily I say unto you, If ye have faith as a grain of mustard seed, ye shall say unto this mountain, Remove hence to yonder place; and it shall remove; and nothing shall be impossible unto you.
> Luke 17:5–6 (Authorized King James Version) states:

Faith, Obedience, and Miracles are Related

> And the apostles said unto the Lord, Increase our faith. And the Lord said, If ye had faith as a grain of mustard seed, ye might say unto this sycamine tree, Be thou plucked up by the root, and be thou planted in the sea; and it should obey you.

Obedience is linked to you be a worker of miracles. When God uses us to release miracles, He is clear with His instructions for answering how, when, where, and what we should do. But He may not give all the details up front like many of us may like. God is precise about our role in the manifestation of miracles, which means we have to have obedient ears and hearts that are ready and willing to carry out the details that He declares—no matter how strange His instructions may sound.

God is notorious for using strange ways to manifest miracles and these are just a few examples of God's ways to perform miracles. He told Elisha, the prophet, to throw salt in a spring of waters in order to heal the waters. God had Elisha tell a widow to borrow jars from her neighbors, then go inside and close the doors behind her and her sons, and then pour the small amount of oil she had into the pots she acquired until they were full. She was then able to sell the jars to make money to live off of after her deceased husband's debts were paid. God told Jesus to heal a blind man by spitting on the ground and mixing His saliva with the dirt to make a mud paste and then place it on a man's eyes. Jesus then told that man to go wash in the Siloam pool. The man was obedient and he came back from the pool able to see.

God can use bizarre means to enact miracles, but the key is to go with His flow the moment He directs you. Don't question God's peculiarity. Just intently listen and obey what He says. When we obey God's instructions while working miracles, we will experience remarkable results, which are God's expected results. When we don't follow His specific instructions, we run into problems, just like Moses did in Numbers 20.

The newer generation of the Israelites started complaining that Moses brought them to another wilderness, the desert of Zin, on their fortieth year in the wilderness encounter. The Israelites fumed with anger toward Moses and Aaron and they tore into them by scolding, blaming, and rebuking them both for taking them to that desert with no water in sight. Moses and Aaron fell on their faces before the Lord and asked Him what to do. The Lord gave them specific details to produce a miraculous supply of water for the people to drink.

Numbers 20:7–8 (Holman Christian Standard Bible) states:

> The Lord spoke to Moses, "Take the staff and assemble the community. You and your brother Aaron are to speak to the rock while they watch, and it will yield its water. You will bring out water for them from the rock and provide drink for the community and their livestock."

God gave Moses very precise instructions of how this miracle should be performed. Moses was supposed to take his staff and go back to the company of people with Aaron and speak to the rock so it could yield the amounts of water that everyone needed. God was specific in that He wanted the camp of Israelites to watch Moses and Aaron speak to a rock. He wanted them to watch water flow out in great volumes to provide for all of them, including their livestock. That series of tasks for the miracle was very important to God because He wanted them to see and know that He was their source of every provision they needed, despite anything negative they thought or were taught by the former generation of Israelites. God wanted them to see how real He was.

After hearing God's instructions, this is what Moses did, in which Aaron was complicit:

> Numbers 20: 9–13 (Holman Christian Standard Bible) states:
> So Moses took the staff from the Lord's presence just as He had commanded him. Moses and Aaron summoned the assembly in front of the rock, and Moses said to them, "Listen, you rebels! Must we bring water out of this rock for you?" Then Moses raised his hand and struck the rock twice with his staff, so that a great amount of water gushed

out, and the community and their livestock drank. But the Lord said to Moses and Aaron, "Because you did not trust Me to show My holiness in the sight of the Israelites, you will not bring this assembly into the land I have given them." These are the waters of Meribah, where the Israelites quarreled with the Lord, and He showed His holiness to them.

Dealing with the generations of rotten thinkers, doubters, and disbelievers for forty years got under Moses' skin. A spirit of offense had clearly built up in his heart and he didn't release that offense, so when the Israelites chastised him, he allowed his anger to delude him in the steps God wanted followed. Moses was angry and he gave the Israelites a piece of his mind by rebuking them before performing a miracle. That is when Moses made his mistake by being disobedient to God. Then, after Moses called the Israelites out for their ways, he struck the rock with his staff twice when God only told him to speak to the rock. In a previous miracle, God told Moses to strike a rock and God caused water to spring forth. God wanted Moses to speak to the rock, so God could show Himself as holy and mighty to all the Israelites. God knew that if He had Moses speak to the rock, there would be a fresh awakening of the hearts of the Israelites.

Moses made some grave mistakes that many of us make. He wanted to avenge himself for how he was treated over a forty-year period. Moses may have been mentally and physically worn out and also annoyed by the constant bickering and displeasure displayed by the generations of the Israelites in the wilderness. Moses already felt he was burdened by their behavior and wanted recompense, an apology, something to feel validated, and he released his anger against the people and more importantly disobeyed God. Moses lost faith that God would take care of the situation for him, and that he wouldn't have to take matters into his own hands. That, too, is where we go wrong. Sometimes, this is a cycle in our lives that happens until we pass the test, let go, and let God handle the problem.

Aaron disobeyed because he was with Moses when God gave them their command. Aaron clearly saw that Moses was angry, and the minute Moses yelled at the Israelites, Aaron could've stopped Moses from going forward with a different plan than the Lord instructed. That is similar to what happened in the Garden of Eden with Adam and Eve. Adam and Eve disobeyed God, and Adam was complicit to Eve's actions when he had the authority to intervene. That level of disobedience was met with God's punishment because God could no longer trust them to be His entrusted ambassadors. Moses and Aaron no longer upheld God's holy nature before the people they served and cared for, and God stripped them of their guarantee of entering the Promised Land.

What happened with Moses and Aaron shows obedience versus disobedience. Since I first read it, it stuck with me. It is embedded in my heart and mind because what Moses and Aaron did is treacherous territory that we should not travel. It should be our desire to please God at all times, even when we get angry. The Bible tells us it's okay to be angry, but we can't let our anger go unchecked or let the sun go down on our anger. We cannot carry it over into the next situation or the next day. We may experience anger, but we must run to God so He can deal with our brokenness. When we feel anger creep in, we have to pause and deal with it, especially when we are on assignment from the Lord, so we don't contaminate or decry God's holiness.

I will leave this chapter with this picture of obedience from Acts 9. There's value in listening to the Lord, asking Him questions, and completing His assignments even if your flesh doesn't like what He has said, or you lack the full spiritual understanding for the mission:

> Acts 9:10–19 (English Standard Version) states:
> Now there was a disciple at Damascus named Ananias. The Lord said to him in a vision, "Ananias." And he said, "Here I am, Lord." And the Lord said to him, "Rise and go to the street called Straight, and at the house of Judas look for a man of Tarsus named Saul, for behold, he is praying, and he has seen in a vision a man named Ananias come in and lay his hands on him so that he might regain his sight." But Ananias answered, "Lord, I have heard from many about

Faith, Obedience, and Miracles are Related

this man, how much evil he has done to your saints at Jerusalem. And here he has authority from the chief priests to bind all who call on your name." But the Lord said to him, "Go, for he is a chosen instrument of mine to carry my name before the Gentiles and kings and the children of Israel. For I will show him how much he must suffer for the sake of my name." So Ananias departed and entered the house. And laying his hands on him he said, "Brother Saul, the Lord Jesus who appeared to you on the road by which you came has sent me so that you may regain your sight and be filled with the Holy Spirit." And immediately something like scales fell from his eyes, and he regained his sight. Then he rose and was baptized; and taking food, he was strengthened.

If Ananias hadn't obeyed God, then Saul, who God changed his identity to Paul, would not have been able to fulfill his destiny in leaving a legacy of believers in Jesus Christ, like you and me. May you marinate on your obedience with the Lord and make a wise choice.

Chapter 10
Miracles Performed by Jesus

Jesus' First Miracle

Throughout the New Testament, there are many miracles that Jesus performed. This chapter will highlight a few of the many miraculous instances and what we can glean from Jesus' ministry.

Jesus' first miracle happened when God commissioned Him to go forth in His ministry call. A few days after officially beginning his ministry, Jesus' mother summoned Him to perform a miracle of turning more than 160 gallons of water into wine at the wedding they attended in Cana of Galilee. Jesus' mother, Mary, nudged on the performance of miracles before Jesus' time had come to work any miracles.

John 2: 1–5 (Authorized King James Version) states:

> And the third day there was a marriage in Cana of Galilee; and the mother of Jesus was there: and both Jesus was called, and his disciples, to the marriage. And when they wanted wine, the mother of Jesus saith unto him, They have no wine. Jesus saith unto her, Woman, what have I to do with thee? mine hour is not yet come. His mother saith unto the servants, Whatsoever he saith unto you, do *it*.

Jesus knew that, eventually, through his ministry that He would perform miracles, but He also knew that was not the time for His first miracle to be performed. Jesus understood God's timing and it wasn't God who instructed

Jesus to reveal his gift of working miracles, it was His mother. Jesus told her that it was not His time to perform, but Mary disregarded what He said and instead told the servants at the wedding to simply do whatever Jesus told them to do.

Although God allowed this miracle of turning water into wine, the full purpose of a miracle wasn't recognized by anyone other than the wedding servants who participated in Jesus' commands and the disciples because that first miracle happened before the destined timing of God. Remember that miracles are aligned with God's purpose and Jesus' response to His mother indicates that replenishing the supply of wine by working a miracle was not part of the destined purpose God had, but it did meet a request made by the mother of Jesus. Miracles should draw attention to who God is to His people. Through miracles, God proves who He is and on that occasion of Jesus turning water into wine, it made the disciples believe and realize who Jesus really was even though they should have already known who He was.

That first miracle performed by Jesus, at the request of His mother, is a lesson to be gleaned about not feeling pressured to produce a miracle or a healing, or other miraculous work outside of timing just because you are familiar with the person requesting a working of miracles. We should be careful to abide by the timing of the Lord and not the timing of man. At the wedding in Cana of Galilee, the ruler of the wedding feast and the wedding party and guests had no recollection that a miracle was performed to keep their taste buds quenched. They simply regarded it as delightful and succulent wine that had not been watered down at the time of the feast where the wine is generally watered down.

God did, in fact, do something even more spectacular at that wedding. He preserved the timing of the revelation of who Jesus was, the Messiah, in front of the company of attendees despite the fervor of Mary's request. We must honor and respect God's timing for how and when He uses us, regardless of who instruct us otherwise.

Woman Healed of Blood Issue

During Jesus' ministry, there was time when He traveled by ship and went to different cities surrounding the Sea of Galilee to perform miracles in front of the numerous people that He encountered. At one time, Jesus traveled by ship into Capernaum and was met at the shoreline by a swell of people. It seemed everywhere He went, the crowds grew larger and larger because word traveled about the miracles, healings, and deliverances He performed in the other cities He visited. One of the rulers of the synagogue, named Jairus, waited there for Jesus because he had a desperate need and enough faith to believe in what Jesus could do. Jairus fell at Jesus' feet as soon as they hit the sand.

Jairus had a twelve-year-old daughter who was sick and at the point of death, and he requested that Jesus go to his home to lay hands on her. Jesus agreed with the request to heal Jairus' daughter and walked with him to get to his house, but the crowd of people engulfed Him. In the midst of the crowd, there was a woman who made her way into the interior of the crowd because she was determined and knew if she could just touch the fringe of Jesus' clothes, she would receive her healing from twelve years of nonstop vaginal bleeding. As soon as the woman touched Jesus' garments she was instantly healed while He simultaneously felt healing virtue leave His body and it made Him turn around to see who received that impartation of His restorative power.

The Bible describes the woman's condition as being unclean according to Levitical law and it is no wonder that she decided to press in from behind Jesus in an attempt to go unnoticed. She was hoping to be healed and go about her way, but Jesus stopped in his tracks to address what He noticed just happened. When Jesus stopped, so did the crowd of people. Although the woman was an outcast because of her impure status, which deemed her or anyone she touched to be unclean, Jesus illuminated her before the large crowd. He asked the crowd which one of them touched His clothes. The woman was afraid, but she went and worshipped at His feet and told Jesus all about her chronic disorder and the money she spent going from doctor to doctor to be healed. She told Jesus how she was destitute and when she heard about the "man called Jesus" she knew she had to make her way to wherever He was, despite what the Levitical law dictated, so she could touch just a portion of His clothing. She told Jesus she knew her decision and her action would result in her receiving healing.

Jesus responded to the woman with such love and compassion. He told her that her faith in who He was and for what she believed the outcome would be, made her whole. Her faith in Jesus restored her to a new, favorable, and healthy condition, and with that she could also have peace. Jesus healed her and gave her a precious gift of peace for all she endured. She didn't expect anything else but to be healed of the bleeding, but Jesus wanted her to experience more than healing. He wanted her to live her days believing in Him and feeling indescribable peace after all the years she lived in torment of being an outcast to her peers. What an awesome blessing.

Jesus is still able to do this, and more, for each of us. There is no limit to what He can do or the miracles He can perform on our behalf. All we have to do is put our faith and trust in Him and then let Jesus minister to us through healing, deliverance, miracles, and so more.

Talitha Cumi

Jairus was a well-known religious leader of the synagogue in Capernaum. As a religious official in that time, Jairus should have opposed anything linked to Jesus because Jesus drew in large crowds everywhere He went and because He disregarded the synagogues stance on not performing miracles on the Sabbath. Jairus was one of the few Jewish leaders who held a holy reverence for Jesus. Despite Jairus' position as the ruler of the synagogue, he humbled himself before Jesus when he made the plea to have Jesus go with him to his home to heal his dying daughter. Jairus had faith in what Jesus could do for his daughter.

While Jesus addressed the woman with the blood issue, someone came to the crowd of people and reported that Jairus' daughter had died, and that Jesus was too late. Let me say this, Jesus is never late to anything. When Jesus heard the report, he told Jairus to not be afraid but only believe. Jesus was not concerned about man's timing, or the report given to Him. His response should encourage us to continue believing in what we've asked despite what the situation looks like in front of us. Jairus had a decision to make and so do we. When we stop believing and operating in faith we tend to miss out on the answers to our prayers. Jairus chose to stay the course, continue believing and walking with Jesus.

The miracle that Jesus performed for Jairus' daughter required faith, so He only permitted three of his disciples, Peter, James, and James' brother John to go with Him to Jairus' house. There were professional moaners and groaners in the home, which were spirits of doubt and disbelief. Jesus, in essence, told them to stop all their weeping because Jairus' daughter was sleeping and not dead. The weepers thought Jesus' words to be funny and they mocked Him, undoubtedly because they had seen and touched the girl's body as their proof and their right to begin their mourning duties before Jesus had even arrived. The weepers were obviously irreverent of who Jesus was and had no respect for His authority, which happens quite today. Jesus' remedy to their behavior was that He put them out of Jairus' house because He knew their presence would not be conducive to the level of faith, quietness, and reverence desired in the daughter's room.

When the environment was clear and full of faith represented by Jairus, his wife, the three disciples, and Jesus, Jesus took the daughter's hand and said Talitha Cumi, which means "Little girl, I say to you, arise." Immediately, the twelve year old girl rose up from the dead and walked out of her room into the view of the very ones who mocked Jesus. Her appearance put the professional mourners in a trance-like state of bewilderment as they were astonished by what they witnessed. When miracles happen in front of the doubters, mockers, and unbelievers, it causes great astonishment, wonder, and amazement to come upon them.

Jesus could have healed the little girl when He was in the swell of the crowd and dealing with the woman with the blood issue, but He wanted an important lesson about belief and faith to be realized even through the report of someone else about the condition of the girl. That is imperative for us to understand. We can receive a negative report, but it doesn't mean that we have to embrace it as God's truth. We can take the situation and the associated report to Jesus through our prayers and request a miracle and hold onto the faith that God will answer in His timing. Jairus believed in Jesus, and he exercised his tremendous faith even when gloominess appeared. Jairus held onto Jesus' words and trusted His timing.

This portion of scripture reminds me of an experience I encountered during a weekend in 2016 when I attended an Aglow Women's Conference. The theme of that conference was based on Isaiah 60:1, which states, "Arise, shine, for your light has come, and the glory of the Lord shines over you." During one of the conference sessions, a minister spoke about the story of Jairus' daughter—in particular—the minister highlighted that God wanted to heal the broken and wounded twelve-year-old girl in each of the attendees. We were instructed to think back on our twelve-year-old selves and recall what may have occurred during that time that caused brokenness to take hold, causing dreams and aspirations to die.

I did as the minister instructed, and I remembered my pre-teen self and the things that happened during that time of my life. I remembered feeling abandoned by dad because of his death and feeling confused, scared, rejected, and hurt. As I stood in the conference room that day, I laid my hands on my stomach during that time of ministry and began to shout out Talitha Cumi as the minister directed.

Talitha Cumi!
Talitha Cumi!
Talitha Cumi!

On that day, I asked God to heal me of the wounds, hurt, and the associated fatigue that plagued me up to that point. The Holy Spirit was present, and I know Jesus interceded on my behalf because within a few minutes I felt the lightest I ever felt in my life. It was like I was riding on a cloud in up in the air. I envisioned Jesus holding my hand and us walking together through a field of fragrant, beautiful flowers and enjoying our time together. Seeing that vision made me cry to know I was with Him, the One who loves me and desires that I be made whole. It made me cry to know that He didn't forsake me and take me for granted. Jesus made me feel just as special as He says I am.

Whatever was dormant in the pit of my stomach was instantly released and eradicated from me, and immediately I was set free from years of internal turmoil and demonic attack. The fatigue I experienced prior to going to the conference was gone. The fatigue was lifted off me in such a manner that my mere words to describe the experience can't do it any justice. All I know is that Jesus healed me that day when I said the words "Talitha Cumi, little girl arise."

Like Jairus' daughter, I rose and was able to take the steps to the next part of my life's journey.

Chapter 11
LIFE APPLICATION: PERSONAL MIRACLE NO. 3

Jesus Healed Me

JESUS DIVINELY HEALED me a few times in my life, and other times directed me toward the steps and processes for healing and deliverance. One significant memory, I experienced divine healing in my late twenties.

One day, I went for a regular gynecology appointment and had a follow-up pap smear test done and other visual examination of my cervix. I remember the doctor told me that I had cancerous cells on my cervix and the pap smear needed to be examined again. I blocked out everything else he said. All I heard was cancer.

The pap smear was sent off to a lab to be evaluated for any additional abnormal findings and confirmation of what the doctor visually noted on my cervix. Once the results were sent back to my gynecologist's office, I would be called to schedule a return appointment so the gynecologist could go over the results with me.

When I left the gynecologists office that day, I was numb. I cried and felt helpless. I was only twenty-six years old and all I could think was that I hadn't even had the opportunity to get pregnant and have a child. I went to my mother's house and told her what happened at the gynecologist office. I cried and cried some more while she listened and attempted to calm me down. My mother then gave me one of the best sets of perceptive instructions a parent can give a child. She told me, "When you go home tonight, kneel down by your bed, and talk to God as if He is right there in the room with you. Tell Him what is going on."

I left and went home and that night. I knelt by my bed and prayed to the Lord. I told God what I encountered and how I felt about it. I told Him I didn't want cancerous cells and that I wanted to be able to have a baby through my womb. When I finished, I got into bed and laid down on my back with my eyes closed. Within a few seconds, I felt a surge and a tingling sensation run from the top of my head down to the soles of my feet. I took note of it and didn't move. Then, I heard the voice of the Lord say to me, "Everything is going to be okay." Hearing His voice didn't scare me, but it made me open my eyes to see where the voice came from. I knew instantly that Jesus spoke to and healed me. I slept peacefully that night.

Two weeks later, I returned to the gynecologist's office to get the lab results from the pap smear. The doctor told me to have a seat in one of the chairs that was situated in front of his desk. The doctor sat in his chair behind his desk, and we faced each other. I waited patiently to hear what the doctor was going to say, but he seemed to be perplexed. He flipped through my chart notes and then looked at me. He did that four times, flipping the pages and then looking at me. I sat there waiting, but inside I was ecstatic because I knew what Jesus did for me just two weeks prior.

Finally, the doctor said, "I don't understand. The results show nothing is wrong, but there were cancerous cells there." I smiled and said, "I know what happened. Jesus healed me." He looked at me, still confused, while I smiled from ear to ear. He released me and I couldn't wait to get out of his office because I felt a shout bubbling up in me. I had to rush to my car to let it out. When I got near my car, which was parked in the parking garage of the hospital, I shouted out loud "Hallelujah, hallelujah, hallelujah!" I couldn't even get in my car because the praise just kept coming out. I was so grateful for the evidence of what I already knew took place. The evidence that indicates faith in the unseen before it even becomes evident in the natural.

All healings are miraculous, but I must admit there is something extraordinary when Jesus touches your body, and you are aware of His touch and the divine healing.

Chapter 12
Miracles are Part of Your Purpose

Miracle Workers

DID YOU KNOW that there are people in this world, in your state, city, and neighborhood who God has assigned to you, and they may be waiting on you to perform miracles on their behalf? Who me, you ask? Yes, you.

Being a miracle worker is something that isn't talked about much when a person accepts Jesus as their Lord and Savior. It's possibly an area of walking with the Lord that many may feel is not suitable conversation for a new convert. Once a person has evolved in their walk with the Lord, identifying with that part of a ministry call has seemed to be relegated only to those in recognized churches or to people with labeled leadership roles. It's not a topic that many groups of friends and family members sit around and discuss at their dinner tables or during family functions. At least that hasn't been my experience.

One of the true spiritual realities of why you walk on the earth in the likeness of Jesus and God the Father is to do more exploits than Jesus himself did. You and I were created to perform miracles in front of those who God has already predetermined to receive His timely and purpose-filled signs and wonders.

During the three years of Jesus' time on earth, He only covered a portion of the ground to perform miraculous works. He was effective in training the disciples and then imparting His spirit so they could cover the rest of the earth, spreading the gospel's good news and performing miracles amongst those they encountered. Jesus Himself said that those who know Him will do greater works than He did. He destined us to be workers of miracles in John 14:8–14 (English Standard Version), which states:

> Philip said to him, "Lord, show us the Father, and it is enough for us." Jesus said to him, "Have I been with you so long, and you still do not know me, Philip? Whoever has seen me has seen the Father. How can you say, 'Show us the Father'? Do you not believe that I am in the Father and the Father is in me? The words that I say to you I do not speak on my own authority, but the Father who dwells in me does his works. Believe me that I am in the Father and the Father is in me, or else believe on account of the works themselves. "Truly, truly, I say to you, whoever believes in me will also do the works that I do; and greater works than these will he do, because I am going to the Father. Whatever you ask in my name, this I will do, that the Father may be glorified in the Son. If you ask me anything in my name, I will do it.

When Jesus' time came to walk in His ministry call, which included performing miracles, He was first commissioned and baptized in water. During His water baptism, the Holy Spirit descended upon Him to empower Him for the enablement of conducting healings, deliverances, casting out of demons, and the working of miracles. The same is true for us. We can't do God's miracles without first acknowledging Jesus as Lord and Savior and knowing that when we pray in His name, we also recognize that God the Father is with Jesus and within us. We must comprehend that we do nothing of our own accord, power, or strength. All the greater works we will do are done through the power and strength of God and through the Holy Spirit that dwells within us. None of the greater works we are to do will ever outshine Jesus or cause us to rise above Him because no one can receive more power than Jesus, and that is not our purpose to do so. To attempt to attain greater power than Jesus should not be desired unless we aspire to be like

Satan. Jesus will empower us to continue on in the great works that He began, and we will do that in His name, the wonderful name of Jesus.

So, what are the works that Jesus did that we are to carry on? The works of Jesus embodied all manners of healings of sickness, infirmities, and disease, which included cleansing lepers and repairing and restoring severed body parts. His works involved casting out demons, raising the dead, and delivering people from Satan's works. Jesus controlled the elements, such as the wind and the water, by walking on the water and calming storms. Jesus manifested anything in the material (natural) and the spiritual realms that aligned with the will of God the Father.

Jesus made provision for us that when He resurrected His life from the dead and left the earth realm for this designated time, He asked the Father, on our behalf, to leave us a dynamic gift, which is the Holy Spirit. That is revealed through the following scriptures:

> John 14:15–20 (English Standard Version)
> "If you love me, you will keep my commandments. And I will ask the Father, and he will give you another Helper, to be with you forever, even the Spirit of truth, whom the world cannot receive, because it neither sees him nor knows him. You know him, for he dwells with you and will be in you. "I will not leave you as orphans; I will come to you. Yet a little while and the world will see me no more, but you will see me. Because I live, you also will live. In that day you will know that I am in my Father, and you in me, and I in you.
> John 14:25–26 (English Standard Version)
> "These things I have spoken to you while I am still with you. But the Helper, the Holy Spirit, whom the Father will send in my name, he will teach you all things and bring to your remembrance all that I have said to you.

Jesus is our intercessor. He makes intercessions for us, which means He goes to God the Father on our behalf for everything. Jesus knew we needed the Holy Spirit's help to be able to continue learning spiritual things of God, encountering, and casting out demons, and performing healings and miracles. Jesus knew what we needed to keep moving forward to bring in the harvest because He too needed the Holy Spirit.

Now that you have read those scripture verses and understand that you were created and born in the likeness of Jesus Christ and are to do greater works than Him, you should be able to grasp that you are a minister of the gospel. With the spreading of the gospel comes the ministry of miracles, signs, and wonders. Don't get hung up on the word "minister," as many religious-minded people view ministers. The word "minister" means you and I were set apart to tend to the people who belong to God. We tend to the care of His lost sheep by advocating for the Kingdom of God as His ambassadors, speaking His truths to tear down strongholds that may have captured them, and using our Holy Spirit given gifts to heal, deliver, and set free those in bondage. Everyone who acknowledges Jesus as Lord is called to be His minister and ambassador.

Before you were born, God selected you to be part of His Kingdom, as His representative, and He designated people to you who He expects you to show up and be present for to ensure they hear a message of salvation and receive healing and deliverance as He wants. He chose you to work with the Holy Spirit to accomplish His divine will. Have you ever wondered why you may run into someone at a store, or a street corner, and you have an internal urge to say a kind word or bless them with food or money? What about the times that someone at work had a rough day and you felt an internal leading to pray for them right there in the work setting and didn't care who saw you? There are many instances that I am certain you could think about right now that show how divine God really is and how He has used you to minister to someone else. There may be times when God placed you on someone else's path so they could tend to your natural or spiritual needs. There are many people on our path during our lifetime that God destined for us to divinely intercept them with healing, deliverance, and miracles.

There is so much that God designed for us to do in our lifetimes. Since we know that a portion of our God-given purpose is to be a worker of miracles, we must make sure that we are always accessible to God for His Kingdom use. We must be sensitive to His movement and be responsive to the leading of the Holy Spirit, so we can fully encounter the people God sends our way. The people that He knows He has equipped you to impart His gospel and His miracles into. We must walk with God, like Moses did, and be ready and available to partner with Him to work the miracles that God designs. Like Moses, we have to accept that we work for the Kingdom of God at all times, and we give ourselves to His beck and call of duty. God's call of duty may lead us to a hospital to lay hands on the sick, to a meeting room to speak and declare a miracle on someone's behalf, to an airport to impart the goodness of God, to someone's home to cast out a demon, or to endless other places. So, let's get to work for the Kingdom of God.

When Moses partnered with God he was afraid, but he didn't allow fear to stop his movement or his obedience. Moses, Jesus, Elijah, Elisha, the apostles, and countless others have answered God's call and so should we. Answer the call to partner with God because people are waiting on the miracles God destined you to perform on their behalf.

Chapter 13
LIFE APPLICATION: PERSONAL MIRACLES PERFORMED

Creative Miracles through Laying on of Hands

IN MY LATE twenties, the Lord used me to perform creative miracles on a few women He loved. They were women who either had trouble conceiving or had experienced miscarriages and had petitioned God for children. God assigned those women to me, to meet with them separately on unique occasions to lay hands on them, pray over them, and minister the working of miracles.

One of the women had trouble conceiving and was told she had polycystic ovarian syndrome (PCOS), which is a condition that can interrupt the reproductive, hormonal balance especially as it relates to ovulation and levels of progesterone needed to conceive. One Sunday, I attended the church that she attended. At some point during the church service, the Lord led me to lay my hands on her bare belly while she sat on the pew. I prayed and spoke in tongues over her womb. I completed my purposed assignment by partnering with the Lord so He could produce a miracle on her behalf. Shortly after that occurrence, the woman and her husband conceived and had a healthy, beautiful daughter, and then later another baby.

Another woman had suffered a series of miscarriages and was distraught and desperately wanted to be able to have a baby. Her and I, along with several other women, were in a home prayer group and she laid on the floor. The Lord told me to go lay hands on her belly, and when I did I prayed in tongues for the manifestation of a healed and healthy womb. About sixty seconds into praying in tongues, I felt a kick against my hand that came from the inner parts of the woman's abdomen. She wasn't pregnant at this time, but I knew it was the Lord's response about the miracle He performed. I said, "I just felt the baby kick. You will be getting pregnant." All of us in the room praised the Lord and cried. We experienced a miracle that day. That woman and her husband conceived and gave birth to a handsome and healthy son and a few years later a beautiful daughter.

The last woman of note already had a son, but she wanted more children and was having difficulty conceiving. One day, A friend and I went to visit her. The Lord told me to pray for her regarding her issue. I went to her home and spoke with her about her desire and asked permission to pray for her and lay hands on her abdominal area. She agreed. I prayed in tongues and spoke things over her concerning her getting pregnant. When I finished, I told her to believe that God would bless her with more children. A few years later, her and her husband conceived and found out they were having twins. She gave birth to a beautiful set of twin daughters. God gave her double for her troubles.

While Visiting in the Hospital

One day I received a phone call from a friend who relayed to me that another friend was in the hospital and asked if I would go to the hospital and pray over her. The hospital she was at happened to be a few blocks away from where I lived. I arrived at the hospital and the friend who called me was already there. The friend who was in the hospital bed seemed happy to see me. We talked a bit so I could find out more about her condition. We all entered into prayer, and I as I prayed, binding up and loosing from Heaven, I laid hands on her and anointed her with oil. I prayed for the hospitalized roommate, too. Within two days, the friend was released from the hospital and later reported to me that "God sent you to heal me."

Miracles Through Speaking in Tongues

God is so amazing for teaching me that even while we sleep and are in the middle of a dream, miracles can be performed. There is an interactive component of the spiritual realm we can experience while sleeping and dreaming that allows us to perform exploits and miracles while simultaneously bringing the miracles performed in the spiritual realm (dream state) into the natural realm.

One night, I slept and had a dream that my mother had a huge lump in her breast. In the dream, the lump was visible to me. I could see my mother crying in the dream. After witnessing that, I woke up and prayed in tongues for my mother and the removal of the lump. I even laid hands on myself at the position where I saw the lump on my mother in the dream and commanded it to leave her.

A few months later, unbeknownst to me, my mother had a spot in her breast that needed to be examined. I hadn't revealed to her the dream I had about the lump I saw on her breast, but my mother had a mammogram that revealed something that she would need to have surgically removed. My mother called me to ask me to go with her to the hospital for the surgical procedure. After examination, the doctors determined that what they saw on the mammogram was fatty tissue and not any cancerous lumps.

God miraculously moved upon my mother and her health scare. He gave me a dream in which I responded to through prophetic prayer and intercession in my heavenly language, my tongues the Holy Spirit poured out on me, and caused the lump in my dream to be removed. God will have you do exploits even while you are in a dream state. Praise God for His healing and miraculous power.

Chapter 14
Miracles are Kingdom Minded

Kingdom Mindset

GOD CREATED MANKIND with the opportunity to exercise free will daily. We can make decisions without consulting the Lord on any matter, whether big or small. Free will can be good, but it also has the capacity to interrupt the perfect will of God. His will for us includes us being obedient to His words and instructions in whatever He has decreed through His decisions, wisdom, creativity, knowledge, and His overall holiness. As believers and partners with God, through Jesus, we should always want to please God and follow His will for our lives and the lives of those we are destined to impact. That is the sole reason we should aspire to have a Kingdom of God mindset.

God's word tells us many times that we are to adopt and take on His mindset because His thoughts are far greater and wiser than our own human thinking. Philippians 2 tells us that we should have the mind of Jesus Christ within us if we are His believers. The loins of our mind must stay girded up and we are to operate with a sound mind according to His word in 1 Peter 1 and 2 Timothy 1. Those of us who believe in God and have accepted Jesus Christ as our Savior as the only way to the Father God must understand that our minds are to be grafted into His Kingdom and we must do what Jesus did, the full and complete will of Father God, which encompasses how we think every day.

There are many mindsets that get in the way of God's plan and His will for our lives. For example, the Pharisee mindset, the Nicolaitan mindset, and the Herodian mindset to name a few. When someone relies on a Pharisee mindset, they embrace a religious and traditional framework that says they acknowledge God in practice only. They may be people who go to church because it is the common or religious thing they should do but they haven't allowed God to become personal to them through individualized experience with the Holy Spirit. That type of person gives explanations about things that happen but doesn't embrace the supernatural or allow the true God to give a right now rhema word or response to any situation or predicament. The Pharisee mindset embraces the fear or rejection of man and what man thinks about situations and is disruptive to letting God truly be God.

The Nicolaitan mindset is linked to a religious and traditional mindset, where people operate with the thinking that a person is saved by grace and therefore it doesn't matter how they live their lives. The mindset focuses on false doctrine where the wrong interpretation of the grace of God's teachings, along with misused grace and liberty of Christ, are condoned to fulfill sinful desires. Revelations 2 expresses that Jesus hates the practices of the Nicolaitans. The way of thinking doesn't allow God's power to operate in a person's life.

The Herodian mindset is a way of thinking that completely excludes God from every situation of life and suggests that popular will, politics, a person's strength, and man-made systems are the way to operate. It says that we as people don't need God because we are able to solve our own problems. A Herodian mindset is equivalent to an atheist mindset in that people don't believe God is alive and active in everyday life. This mindset creates the influence that there is no divine intervention, such as miracles, healings, or deliverance that occur every day by the power of God. The Herodian mindset encourages a person to be self-made and function under the sway that discipline and determination will replace anything God can do.

Many of us may have adopted these mindsets at one point or another, especially if we have been part of a church or religious system. These mindsets are highly present today, just as they were in biblical days, and are seemingly easy to flow in and out of without realizing they have dominated our thinking. They erode the power of faith that we need to function in the intimate relationships we are to have with God. Any mindset or adopted way of thinking that limits the power of God in our lives is an evil impediment to our ability to adopt the Kingdom of God way of thinking and living. The key thing now is to recognize the mindset, repent for allowing the mindset to rule over you, and then kick the false mindset out of your mind by telling it that it no longer has reign over you and how you think.

> **Kingdom minded miracles require us to have Kingdom of God mindsets.**

What does that mean?

We, as believers, are not to conform to the world's notions about how to function, what to be, and how to think. We are not to agree with the absurdities and evil that abound in daily living. Our minds are to be transformed and renewed (Romans 12:2) so that we see and hear what God is doing and operate according to His thoughts and precepts. It also means that our thoughts should be downloaded to us from God to ensure we are not thinking our own way. God lets us know that

> **We need a mindset shift so we can be led according to His plan and will.**

Isaiah 55:8–9 (English Standard Version)

> For my thoughts are not your thoughts, neither are your ways my ways, declares the Lord. For as the heavens are higher than the earth, so are my ways higher than your ways and my thoughts than your thoughts.

Our way of thinking contains limits and boundaries that God can surpass in order to achieve His prescribed will. Our way of thinking can be tainted and soiled, which can keep us from operating in Kingdom of God pursuits and exploits. We do have the ability and the authority to cast down every vain, unproductive, and useless imagination and thought that is in opposition with the thoughts and will of God. When we have the God of Heaven directing our thinking and transforming our mindset, He gives us the ability to transcend negative thoughts, doubts, and fears that pollute our mindsets every day. Our faith, coupled with God's thoughts and plans, allow us to move in the miraculous in ways we could never imagine. We are to function like Proverbs 3:5–7 (English Standard Version) instructs:

> Trust in the Lord with all your heart, and do not lean on your own understanding. In all your ways acknowledge him, and he will make straight your paths. Be not wise in your own eyes; fear the Lord and turn away from evil.

When we trust God, we then can stop leaning on ourselves for our own wisdom and understanding that restricts us by putting us in a box that prevents the free flow of the Holy Spirit. If we do what the scripture states, we will find that we put a dependence and reliance on hearing God for all wisdom and answers we need, which then results in built up trust and faith in allowing His thoughts and ways to occupy our minds. Then, we can be like Jesus and do the will of the Father because we would have yielded our minds and hearts to God for His complete use. These are necessary steps in walking the distance with God to positively impact the Kingdom of God as well as performing miracles on His behalf.

When we talk about being prepared and ready to work with God in performing miracles, there is no room to exercise our own will over the will of God. God's will should triumph so that we can remain in order with the miracles God wants to produce through us. Even Jesus understood this spiritual principle, that it was better to adhere to God's will and not his own.

Matthew 7:21–23 (Holman Christian Standard Bible) states:

> Not everyone who says to Me, 'Lord, Lord!' will enter the kingdom of heaven, but only the one who does the will

of My Father in heaven. On that day many will say to Me, 'Lord, Lord, didn't we prophesy in Your name, drive out demons in Your name, and do many miracles in Your name?' Then I will announce to them, 'I never knew you! Depart from Me, you lawbreakers!

John 8:28–29 (Holman Christian Standard Bible) states: So Jesus said to them, "When you lift up the Son of Man, then you will know that I am He, and that I do nothing on My own. But just as the Father taught Me, I say these things. The One who sent Me is with Me. He has not left Me alone, because I always do what pleases Him."

Jesus knew His purpose for His life, and He valued doing the will of God the Father in order to please Him. We should all aim to walk the way Jesus did. We should cherish the ability to please God by consistently being obedient and doing His will. Those who do that, God calls His own.

Prophetic Word about God's People

Recently when I spent time listening to the Lord, I heard Him say, "Burn, Baby Burn." I immediately remembered the 1976 song by the Trammps called *Disco Inferno*. The phrase was also coined in 1965 following the fires in Los Angeles, California, known as the Watts Riots, where businesses and communities were set on fire and the people shouted, "Burn, Baby Burn!"

After hearing God tell me that phrase, I went on YouTube, listened to the popular song, and read the lyrics. The lyrics referred to people being up on a high rooftop and the heat of the inferno being so strong that it ignited everyone ablaze. A burning inferno didn't cause them to literally burn, but one that caused their souls to light up and their individual sparks to get lit. The lyrics stated that the people were screamed out of control, in an entertaining way, shouting the words "Burn, Baby Burn."

Although the song was penned to reflect a scene in a movie displaying a fire on a rooftop disco, God can surely use anything He wants to deliver a message. In that case, the song was a metaphorical analogy of the music on the rooftop raging with such heat the people dancing went ablaze. When I finished listening to the song, I asked the Lord what He meant by the phrase, "Burn, Baby Burn." What exactly was He trying to relay to me? The Lord then told me that

> **He was setting His people ablaze and they would become burning ones for His Kingdom**

and then followed that statement with, "Burn, Baby Burn!"

Burning ones, in the Bible, generally refers to God's fiery angels, the Seraphim, and they represent the holiness of God. Adam was a burning one once God created him and blew the breath of fire into Adam's nostrils. In that breath, God blew the hot kindling breath, which was the spirit of God and the fire of God creating a burning one in the image and likeness of God. God desires burning ones in His Kingdom.

God takes His people from the stages of witnessing the miracle of a fiery flame visitation by God to His people becoming miracle workers and operating in His Kingdom's holiness to set others on a course of heating up the harvest and setting everyone ablaze for their God ordained Kingdom purpose. That is the trajectory God put Moses on during his mission to free the Israelites from bondage in Egypt, which is why the intimate oneness with God is critical and highly valued because exploits of great miracles require the movement of the Kingdom of God's glory.

Chapter 15
Timed Connection of Miracles

Timing of Miracles

An essential theme of time runs through the Bible, as well portions of this book. God is the creator of time, He owns and directs time, and He always accomplishes happenings according to His time and seasons to coincide with His purpose. From the very beginning of time, we can ascertain those miracles are events that are linked to God's timeliness. God showed us this in the first few chapters of Genesis and beyond.

God uses time and seasons to demonstrate what He does in heaven to allow us to make decrees on the earth in response to what He has demonstrated. He shows signs and wonders all around us that are linked to His timed events. God makes use of time to signify when and how we should pray, what we should declare in the atmosphere, and how we should function in time with our relationships with Him. God employs time to facilitate the manifestation of healings, deliverance, blessings, miracles, and much more.

Have you ever wondered why you may not have received an immediate response to a prayer request that you submitted to the Lord? Countless people do not fully comprehend the spiritual concepts of God's time. Many believe that when they have a need or concern that at that very moment God should respond to their need, but His responsiveness to our cry for help does not always manifest with the immediacy we perceive or would like.

There is a concept about delay of time where the natural mind would make one believe that something is being held up from reaching them in a temporal related timetable. Man's clock is linear and recently thought to have an immediate nature and priority based on fleshy desires for when things should happen. God's clock is very different from ours. He can render time eternally, cyclically, temporally, and across a continuum. God knows no bounds and is not subject to the whims we place on time and response.

Psalm 27:14 encourages us to be strong and wait patiently on the Lord while 1 Corinthians 2:14 indicates that we don't understand God's timing and His readiness for administering answers to things we have prayed unless we do so by the Spirit:

> 1 Corinthians 2:14 (English Standard Version)
> The natural person does not accept the things of the Spirit of God, for they are folly to him, and he is not able to understand them because they are spiritually discerned.

God does respond to our prayers, our cries for help, and our pleas for a miracle in a timely manner but we must recognize that His responses and released miracles are delivered based on His divine purpose and His timing. Ecclesiastes 3:1 (Authorized King James Version) states:

> To everything there is a season, and a time to every purpose under the heaven

Ecclesiastes 3 states that there are times for this and times for that. The chapter makes it clear that God operates in time and seasons, and we have to be like the tribe of Issachar (1 Chronicles 12:32), knowing and understanding the time and seasons. If we live without the awareness of how God operates through time and seasons, it restricts us from partnering with Him to bring responsive answers to the cries of challenge. As workers of miracles, we must learn to maneuver with Him, in His timing.

> Ecclesiastes 3:2-8 (Authorized King James Version) states:
> A time to be born and a time to die; A time to plant and a time to uproot what is planted. A time to kill and a time

to heal; A time to tear down and a time to build up. A time to weep and a time to laugh; A time to mourn and a time to dance. A time to throw away stones and a time to gather stones; A time to embrace and a time to refrain from embracing. A time to search and a time to give up as lost; A time to keep and a time to throw away. A time to [a]tear apart and a time to sew together; A time to keep silent and a time to speak. A time to love and a time to hate; A time for war and a time for peace.

Based on Ecclesiastes 3 there are specific, designated times ordained by God for healing that can incorporate deliverance and working of miracles based on the understanding about the gifts of the Holy Spirit in 1 Corinthians 12. So, when we partner with God to perform miracles, we must step into that position knowing that He will direct the miracle to manifest at the precise time He authorizes.

The story of Jesus' birth is a notable example of how God materializes miracles in relation to time and purpose. Jesus is our promised Lord and Savior, the Messiah who was miraculously conceived for a set time and purpose for all of us to benefit. God caused a star to appear in the sky at a set time so it could make an announcement that the promised Messiah was in fact on the earth. The miracle of Jesus' birth had both timing and purpose assigned to it. Jesus came to the earth to teach and lead us into a relationship with Him, offer us salvation and redemption of our sins, heal the sick, cast out demons, work miracles, and many other nameless benefits.

Shortly after Jesus was born, some wise men saw a sign in the sky, which was a specific star that was positioned in an easterly direction. The wise men understood the times and seasons and knew exactly what that star meant. They were prepared to follow the star so they could go before Jesus and worship Him and present Him with gifts of gold, frankincense, and myrrh. One interesting feature about the star is that it miraculously traveled ahead of the wise men, similarly to how the cloud pillar led the Israelites out of Egypt.

The wise men traveled and sought out King Herod to ask him where Jesus was because they saw the appearance of the star. Herod had no idea about the star or Jesus' birth, as Herod was an atheist who did not appreciate anything about God or what He did. Herod questioned the wise men about the exact time they saw the star appear because he wanted to tabulate how old Jesus was to be able to have his army kill Him. The wise men provided an answer with a range of one to two years prior. Herod instructed the wise men to search diligently for Jesus and once they found Him report it back to Herod, claiming he wanted to be able to go and worship Jesus also.

Praise God that throughout the entire encounter, His timing was impeccable and above that which an ungodly man like Herod could interpret. After the wise men found Jesus and worshipped before Him, God gave them a dream that instructed them not to return to Herod and they obeyed. The Bible later notes that unbeknownst to Herod, God sent Jesus and His parents to Egypt by alerting them that Herod was coming to kill Jesus. After a time, Herod realized the wise men ignored his order and he made a mandate to his army that all boys aged two and under were to be slain, which was based on the timing of the star's appearance.

In Acts 16, there is another occurrence of God's timing relative to working miracles. During a mission trip, the Holy Spirit forbade Paul, Luke, Timothy, and others accompanying them to preach the word of God in the territories of Asia Minor, Mysia, and Bithynia for the sole reason that the timing was not right. The Holy Spirit changed Paul and his company's plans because He knew the people in those territories were not ready to receive the preached word and any demonstrations of signs and wonders. Paul had to be in tune with the Holy Spirit to recognize what was shared and to not encroach on the timing of the Lord. Paul allowed the Lord to redirect their mission trip. The Lord gave Paul a vision where a man in the vision told Paul to go into Macedonia. God let Paul know the people in Macedonia were ripe and ready for the preached word and the timed miracles that would take place there. Paul, Timothy, and company were able to stay several days in Macedonia and follow the leading of the Lord, which included casting out demons.

Timed Connection of Miracles

Much can be gleaned by those occurrences about time and God's working of miracles. Time is an eternal event that is at the exclusive discretion of God based on the fulfillment of His purposes for each of us. Those of us who partner with God and obey Him must understand time and seasons and how that relates to God dispersing working of miracles on behalf of His people.

Chapter 16
Partnering with God to Perform Miracles

Partnering with God

MOSES IS ONE of the greatest examples we can look too for guidance about collaborating with the Lord to perform miracles. When Moses was introduced to God, he began his relationship with Him and learned about a portion of the call God ordained for him. In the beginning of their relationship, Moses tested God by continually having a reason why he couldn't do the mission God called him to do. Moses mentioned every shortcoming he could think of, from lacking confidence and boldness, feeling unready and not prepared, to having a problem with his speech, in which God countered every presumed weakness.

Moses discovered that he was to work side by side with the Lord to be a worker of miracles. God enrolled Moses into His individualized training camp so He could bring Moses up to speed on the tasks at hand. During Moses' one-on-one training with the Lord, he grasped that the primary purpose of all miracles, according to Exodus 4:5, is to reveal to people that God is very real and that He can and will appear to address their cares and concerns. Moses made a conscience decision to team up with God on behalf of the people God wanted to rescue. The decision Moses made is the same one that God looks for from us. He wants us to yield and surrender so we can be effective in His Kingdom to perform miracles and exploits on His behalf.

When God calls you to perform miracles, He will register you into His personalized training camp, which requires an agreement from you to be humbly taught and matured. The book of Exodus illustrates the step-by-step engagement that Moses had with God. God taught Moses in an interactive manner where God not only taught about the purpose of the miracles, but God also applied practical demonstration methods that resulted in hands on learning for Moses. That teaching method helped Moses overcome fear of the miracles God would produce in front of him while instilling confidence and endurance for the miraculous tasks that he would perform at God's instruction.

In my late twenties, I went on a walk in an area near my house that had a walking path surrounded by wooded trees. On that day, the Lord talked to me about His resurrection power and the power that Jesus left for me to perform miracles. I came to a portion of the path where I saw a dead mouse laying on the ground. I heard the Lord say to me, "Command the mouse to come back to life." I immediately froze in place because all I could think about was that I was afraid of mice. I hadn't like mice since my pre-teen years and even now I don't care to see them. I also became afraid of having a front row seat of watching the mouse come back to life before my eyes after knowing it was dead on the ground. Needless to say, I didn't do what the Lord asked of me, and I had to ask Him to forgive me.

Now, I understand that I missed my personalized training class that God enrolled me in without me realizing it. I didn't know that God had enrolled me in a miracles boot camp class as He sprung it up on me in the moment of general conversation with Him. I realized that the same must have happened with Moses. Moses and God had a conversation about what God needed Moses to tell the Israelites and then God sprung Exodus 4:2–3 (Authorized Kings James Version) on him:

> And the Lord said unto him, "What is that in thine hand?"
> And he said, "a rod." And he said, "Cast it on the ground."
> And he cast it on the ground, and it became a serpent; and Moses fled from it.

Moses had no idea that his conversation with the Lord would turn into an on-the-spot training experience, and neither did I. Most likely, neither will you. Moses watched that rod turn into a serpent, and it scared him so much that he ran. I, on the other hand, froze and didn't open my mouth. God knows our fears and I truly believe that He had me encounter a training on miracles that included the faith to overcome one thing that would make me run. If we can stay the course of the teaching, we can then advance to the next level of our personalized miracle boot camp trainings. One of the important lessons to remember is to be flexible and go with the flow during the training encounter because God won't let anything bad happen to you. God is bigger than any fear we may have, even if part of the training is to exercise authority over the one thing we fear. For me, hindsight is 20-20, and I welcome my continued training experiences with the Lord. Thankfully, Moses moved onto the next level of his training.

Moses continued in God's miracles boot camp and gained new levels of trust in God. He recognized a key principle about miracles which is that he could not work miracles on his own. Working miracles is one of the gifts presented to us by the Holy Spirit at His will. Moses learned that he must rely on God's strength and not his own. Like Moses, we have to embrace that nothing we do for God, or His Kingdom, is done in our own strength. Our strength is limited no matter how physically or mentally capable we may be. Moses knew he needed the direction of the Holy Spirit to work miracles, and so do we.

Once Moses completed his miracles boot camp training, God was ready to send Moses forth in his assignment, and Moses offended the Lord. Moses finished four guided miracles by God's instruction that prepared him to confront six million Israelites with the word God had for them. The word God was going to release through Moses required manifestation of miracles for all the Israelites to see in order to spark their obedience to flee Egypt at God's command. Moses then asked the Lord to send someone else on the mission and it sparked anger in God. Moses was afraid to go forward and get pulled out of his comfort zone, so he made up another excuse to try to get out of the assignment. Moses met another side of God that day. He met the angry God, which many today don't believe exists, but it does. Moses acted out of a spirit of stubbornness and rebellion, which are very unpleasing to God. Both stubbornness and rebellion can damage our intimate connection with God and prevent the blessings He has for us. Stubbornness is an attitude of great determination to not change a person's mind or position about something, while rebellion is a violent act of resistance to authority and is considered witchcraft in 1 Samuel 15:23 (Authorized King James Version), which states:

> For rebellion is as the sin of witchcraft, and stubbornness is as iniquity and idolatry. Because thou hast rejected the word of the Lord, he hath also rejected thee from being king.

When we reject God and what He calls us to do, He can then reject us from anything He originally planned for us, including blessings, favor, and even knowing us. Playing around with God in that manner is not a wise tactic in trying to get our way. It doesn't work.

In Moses' case, God supplemented the assignment for Moses by including his brother Aaron to assist him in the mission of saving the Israelites, but God still made it clear that Moses would have to be God's spokesman. Moses couldn't outwit and manipulate God, and neither can we. When we are assigned, called, or ordained to a task or mission, the best strategy for us is obedience. We don't want God getting angry with us because of any nonsensical manipulation we may employ. It's not worth it to be on the wrong side of Him.

Once God set Moses straight, he was able to move forward to work with God using the tools of confidence, trust, reliance, and obedience to complete the assigned mission. That strategy is relevant for us in anything that God calls us to, especially miracles. Moses' training taught him that he needed to have an open ear to hear God's instructions, be sensitive and flexible to God's movements, be precise and timely in how he performs, and maintain strict adherence to God's plan. Moses' training taught him to abandon his own feelings or opinions about himself, or what God was doing, because he learned it was a disruptor to being obedient. Moses learned that his mind had to be renewed and transformed to operate the way God does to perform miracles.

When God appoints us to be workers of miracles, He also teaches and prepares us while simultaneously anointing us for each miraculous encounter.

Chapter 17
YOUR MIRACLE JOURNEY

AS YOU HAVE learned, you are a vital link to participating in the pursuit and performance of miracles. God always destined for you to partner with Him as His miracle worker through whatever mode of wondrous transmission He deems from heaven. This is your miracle journey diary, so you can record the miracles you have experienced and the miracles you performed by the power of the Holy Spirit. Take some time to ponder your life and the miracles you recognize. Then be bold enough to tell the Lord that you are ready In order to put space before the table begins please double space after these words "to be His instrument—His miracle worker."

Miracles Personally Expirenced	Miracles Holy Spirit Had Me Perform

Miracles Personally Expirenced	Miracles Holy Spirit Had Me Perform

About the Author

YVETTE J SMITH is a destiny driven author since she first penned her autobiography for a school assignment at age ten to the many poems written and the career professional co-authored journal article. Yvette has been in pursuit of bringing God's inspiration and motivation to the world. She is the insightful and uplifting author of And Hannah Stopped Crying: Biblical Reflections of Purpose, Promise, and Hope for Women Facing Infertility and Still Time for Miracles: Partnering with God to Perform Miracles which bring a new level of Kingdom of God expression to readers everywhere.

Yvette resolutely decided a long time ago to yield her will to the Lord Jesus Christ so she could partner with the Holy Spirit to help equip and train people about walking in their Kingdom of God purpose, which includes healing, deliverance, and miracles. Yvette is a registered nurse, a doula, an ordained pastor, and a prophetic teacher and intercessor that is aligned with Glory of Zion International Ministries.

Yvette resides in Pennsylvania and loves the peace and tranquility of horses, the horizons, and time at the beach. She enjoys gardening, puzzles, movies, and the simple things of life. Yvette looks forward to the continued works that God will produce through her so that His voice can be heard and felt by others worldwide.

ENDNOTES

1. Popernack ML, Gray N, Reuter-Rice K. Moderate-to-Severe Traumatic Brain Injury in Children: Complications and Rehabilitation Strategies. J Pediatric Health Care. 2015;29(3):e1-e7. doi:10.1016/j.pedhc.2014.09.003 Accessed on September 2, 2021, https://www.ncbi.nlm.nih.gov/pmc/articles/PMC4409446/

2. Merriam Webster Dictionary. Definition of Miracle. Accessed on December 4, 2021, https://www.merriam-webster.com/dictionary/miracle

3. EliYah Ministries. Strong's Concordance with Hebrew and Greek Lexicons. Accessed on December 4, 2021, https://www.eliyah.com/lexicon.html

4. Dake M, Dake EF, Germaine M, Kennedy DK, Iglinski KD, and Dake Ministries. Dake's Annotated Reference Bible: The Old and New Testaments, with Notes, Concordance, and Index. 1999.

5. Ibid.

CPSIA information can be obtained
at www.ICGtesting.com
Printed in the USA
BVHW081022041122
651158BV00002B/348